Contents

Introduction

There are around 25 million homes in the UK, and 69% of these are owner-occupied. This means there are over 17 million homeowners in the UK, and the number is rising every year. Less than a fifth of these spend their whole lives in the first property they buy. So over 80% of homeowners will find themselves in the position of selling their house at least once, and some will sell and buy several times during their lifetimes.

Because so many people sell their houses each year, a huge industry has built up around property transactions. Selling a house can be complicated, sometimes takes a long time, and mistakes can be costly. The process can be stressful and full of delays, and is rarely undertaken without help from a whole raft of professionals. Not surprisingly, someone selling a house for the first time can feel bewildered and overwhelmed. If you have never sold a house before, this book can be your guide, and is packed with helpful advice to make the process of selling easier.

On the other hand, if you have sold a house before, but been dissatisfied with the process or the outcome, this book is also for you. You will already have experienced part of the learning curve, but every property sale is unique and it can take several sales before you feel that you qualify as an experienced seller.

When selling a house, there are factors outside your control, such as the number of potential buyers available and the economic climate. But there is much you can do to make the process quicker, easier and more straightforward, and there are also a number of things you can do to affect the speed of your sale and the eventual selling price.

This easy-to-read guide will steer you through the whole process, right from the initial decision to sell, to the completion of the last piece of paperwork. It will look at what you can do before you put your property on the market to attract buyers and maximise the price. The various methods by which a property can be sold will be discussed, along with the paperwork and costs you may encounter. The agencies and individuals you will need to work with as you

- Solicitor (lawyer/property solicitor/conveyancing solicitor)
- Licensed conveyancer
- Online conveyancer
- Solicitor estate agent (Scotland only)

Whilst these people may have slightly different overall job descriptions, they all do conveyancing.

Solicitors

Solicitors are practising lawyers who have had a legal education that may have taken up to 8 years, and have passed examinations that qualify them to carry out legal work on your behalf. They will be qualified to degree level and maybe beyond, and can act in a whole range of legal matters. This means a solicitor will be able to offer you advice on other legal matters that relate to your sale, such as probate, lease extensions and wills.

Someone who calls themselves a property solicitor or a conveyancing solicitor is likely to be a solicitor who specialises in conveyancing. There are specialist legal firms who have a large staff of property/conveyancing solicitors who do this. Although such companies undoubtedly have a mass of expertise in the buying and selling of property, some people prefer to use a local firm of solicitors, who have a detailed knowledge of local properties and who can be visited in person.

Solicitors are regulated by the Law Society and the Solicitors Regulation Authority, and have to abide by a code of conduct. You will not be allowed to use the same solicitor as your buyer, although if there is no conflict of interest, two different solicitors in the same firm may sometimes be used. This is not recommended, however, in case a conflict of interest arises during the transaction.

Licensed conveyancers

Licensed conveyancers have passed examinations that qualify them to act on your behalf solely in matters related to the sale and purchase of property in England and Wales, but they are not necessarily educated in law to degree level. They are regulated by the Council of Licensed Conveyancers and also have to abide by a code of conduct.

Both solicitors and licensed conveyancers have to have professional indemnity insurance, but solicitors generally have a higher level than licensed conveyancers. Also, some mortgage lenders object to conveyancers and insist on a solicitor.

If you are selling a house in Northern Ireland, you will have to use a solicitor, as there they have a monopoly on conveyancing.

Online conveyancers

Online conveyancing is becoming more widely used nowadays. There are certainly some cheap deals on the Internet, but, unless you are acting on the recommendation of a friend who has used one of these services, it will be difficult to know what quality of service to expect.

You should always obtain documentation from online companies that prove they are licensed to provide this service. Be aware that companies that are based outside the UK may not be bound by the same laws as those based within the UK.

'Try to avoid becoming involved with what is known as a "conveyancing factory".'

'Conveyancing factories'

Try to avoid becoming involved with what is known as a 'conveyancing factory'. This is an organisation devoted solely to conveyancing, typically offering competitive rates, and dealing with a high volume of routine transactions.

These companies typically use a higher proportion of unqualified staff and often operate overseas-based call centres, where you are unlikely to ever speak to the same person twice. These organisations do complete successful transactions, but there can sometimes be serious drawbacks to using this type of provider, including the levels of attention to detail, local knowledge and expertise if your sale hits an unexpected legal snag.

Solicitor estate agents

If you are selling a house in Scotland, you have the option to choose a solicitor estate agent who, as the name suggests, will combine the functions of a solicitor and an estate agent. This is a tradition particular to Scotland, and is not available in the rest of the UK. You can also choose to use separate companies or individuals for the two tasks of marketing and conveyancing. Chapter 10 gives further information on sales in Scotland.

Choosing by recommendation

If you were satisfied with the solicitor or conveyancer you used when you bought your house, it might be sensible to go back to that firm again. If not, ask your family and friends for a recommendation. It is usually best to go to a professional who has been recommended by someone who has had personal experience of dealing with them.

Choosing from a directory

The Law Society has a regional directory for solicitors in your area, but will not be able to comment on the quality of service offered. However, it should certainly be a minimum requirement that the solicitor you choose will be in the Law Society's directory.

You might find a solicitor in the telephone directory or a business directory. This is not the best method of choosing, as there is a chance that you will randomly pick someone who is not very good at their job. Also, you are more likely to end up entangled with a conveyancing factory.

So try to get some additional information about the firm. Questions you could ask include:

- Do they do the type of work you need done?

- Where are they based?
- Is there someone within the firm who specialises in conveyancing? If you choose a firm whose solicitors do little conveyancing, you may find your solicitor is in court a great deal, or engaged in other matters that seem to take priority over your house sale.
- What fees are they expecting to charge?

Choosing based on price

Conveyancing fees can vary greatly, but do not be tempted to choose based solely on fees. It is also worth bearing in mind that smaller firms do not necessarily charge less, and that firms that are more expensive are not necessarily more competent.

Never instruct on the basis of a telephone quote, but insist on a written quotation, where the cost is detailed, the terms are clearly laid out, and you can study them at your leisure.

The Law Society of Northern Ireland requires solicitors in that part of the UK to give a written estimate of what their fees are likely to be, or how they will be calculated, along with details of other expenses that may be involved in the transaction.

As well as the cost, consider whether you have found the firm to be pleasant and easy to deal with.

'Conveyancing fees can vary greatly, but do not be tempted to choose based solely on fees.'

What costs are involved in selling a house?

If you are buying another property, it will be tempting to just compare the selling price of your house with the purchase price of the one you want to buy. This is unlikely to give you a realistic figure. It is useful to prepare a selling budget estimating or obtaining quotes for any of the following costs that will apply to your sale:

- Preparing the house for marketing
- Solicitor's/conveyancer's fees
- Disbursements (additional fees incurred during conveyancing)

- Estate agent's fee/auction fee/advertising
- Energy Performance Certificate (see chapter 9)
- Repairs that may be highlighted by the buyer's survey
- Mortgage redemption fees (charged when a mortgage is paid back in full)
- Removal/storage costs
- Negative equity (when your house is worth less than your mortgage)
- Capital gains tax (payable on second homes)
- Final utility bills

If you are buying another house there will be a second set of conveyancing fees and disbursements, and perhaps additional mortgage costs.

What are disbursements?

Disbursements are costs that you may incur as a result of selling your house that are separate from the solicitor's fee. They may include insurances, Land Registry fees, postage and other one-off costs.

Normally, a good solicitor will check with you before incurring expenditure on your behalf, but it will be best to allow for these in your budget.

Remember to add VAT, which may be payable on some of these charges and will definitely be payable on the solicitor's fee.

What is negative equity?

If you bought your house at the peak of the property bubble, it is possible it is now worth less than you paid for it. Land Registry figures show that in 2012 house prices were, on average, 11% lower than they were in 2007. In some areas prices during this period fell by as much as 25%. If you are in the position where the sale price of your house is less than your mortgage, you are in negative equity and this may lead to problems when you try to sell your house.

'If the sale price of your house is less than your mortgage, you are in negative equity and this may lead to problems when you try to sell your house.'

In 2012, The Council of Mortgage Lenders estimated that there were 719,000 UK households in negative equity. The problem is worse in Northern Ireland, affecting maybe as many as one in three households. In other parts of the UK, the worst hit areas are, of course, those where prices are dropping, meaning the problem is greatest in Wales and the North, with London and the south of England being the least affected.

Can I still sell my house if I am in negative equity?

Yes, if you can make up the shortfall between the value of the mortgage and the value of the house.

Many people who cannot do this are sitting it out, hoping that the value of their property will rise once more. But what if you absolutely have to move and you do not have enough savings to cover the difference between the two figures?

The first thing to do is to talk to your mortgage lender. Some lenders will offer you an alternative loan onto which you can transfer, whilst a few lenders allow borrowers to transfer the mortgage to a new property. Much will depend upon your personal circumstances and income.

If you are going to move to a more expensive house, you will still need to find a deposit for the property you are buying. Do not omit to budget for this.

If your lender cannot help you, another option to consider is renting out your house to fund a new home elsewhere. You will need consent from your lender to do this and there may be additional charges involved. You will also need to check with your insurance provider, as a different type of insurance policy is usually required for rented properties.

Capital gains tax

When you sell the house in which you live (your principal private residence, as it is known by the Inland Revenue), you qualify for private residence relief, so there is no capital gains tax to pay. However, if the house you are selling is a second home then, unless your circumstances are very unusual, you will be required to pay capital gains tax on any profit you make on its sale.

The recent furore over Members of Parliament 'flipping' their homes highlights a legal way to avoid this tax, by strategically electing a second home as the principal private residence. This is both an ethical and a legal minefield, and you are best advised to seek sound legal and financial advice if you want to emulate those MPs who appear to have got away with doing this. Do not forget that if you can prove that your second house is your main residence, then your first house will become liable for capital gains tax.

If you have ever used the house for business purposes, you may qualify for capital gains tax relief, and you should seek financial advice.

If you are facing a large capital gains tax bill, you will be well advised to seek expert financial help to assess whether your liability can be reduced.

Summing Up

* Decide who is going to do your conveyancing. The people who can do this work are solicitors, licensed conveyancers, online conveyancers and, in Scotland only, solicitor estate agents. Avoid using any company that might be described as a 'conveyancing factory'.

* The best way to choose a solicitor or conveyancer is by recommendation. Always get a written quotation, but beware of selecting only on the basis of the fees quoted. Never hire on the basis of a telephone quote only.

* Prepare a budget of the expected costs of the house sale. These may include preparing the house for sale, solicitor and estate agent fees, negative equity, Energy Performance Certificate, mortgage redemption costs, and final utility bills and removal costs.

* If the house you are selling is a second home, it is likely that you will be liable to pay capital gains tax on its sale.

Chapter Two

What is my House Worth?

No house has a fixed, absolute value. Property prices rise and fall, and areas fluctuate in popularity. Your house can increase in sale value if a new rail link opens nearby, or it can fall in sale value if your local airport decides to build a new runway at the end of your garden.

The value placed on your house by your insurance company is the cost of rebuilding it in the event of it being damaged or destroyed. This figure usually bears no relation to the market value.

Equally, the price you paid for your house is not necessarily an indicator of its present sale value.

Tomorrow your house may not be worth what it is worth today. Prices in your area are likely to be rising or falling: only rarely do property prices remain static.

The sale value of a property consists simply of the amount a buyer is willing to pay and the seller is willing to accept. If you ask three estate agents to value your property for selling purposes, you may well be given three different opinions.

'The sale value of a property consists simply of the amount a buyer is willing to pay and the seller is willing to accept.'

Economic factors

Everybody knows that house prices fluctuate. In the last few decades they tended to mainly rise and people who bought property could expect it to increase in value steadily, and sometimes rapidly. However, since prices peaked in 2007, it has been a very different story and many homes are now losing value.

The fall in house prices has been made worse by the current difficulty of obtaining mortgages, especially for first-time buyers. It is widely predicted that the £130 billion package aimed at helping first-time buyers announced in the government's budget in early 2013, together with historically low interest rates, will revive the flagging property market. If this happens, it is likely to result in an increase in numbers of house sales, and a boost to property prices.

Buyer's and seller's markets

When times are good, unemployment is low and mortgages are easy to obtain, more people want to buy houses. Buyers outnumber sellers, who may find themselves in the happy position of receiving multiple offers. All this activity and competition pushes up house prices. This is known as a seller's market.

Unfortunately, at the time of writing, many parts of the UK are in a buyer's market. Times are hard, unemployment is high and it is tough to find a mortgage. Sellers outnumber buyers and house prices are generally flat. Estate agents are telling sellers that they are lucky to receive an offer, and they should think about accepting, even if it is lower than hoped.

What else affects the sale price?

Economic factors aside, there are five main factors that affect the sale value of your house:

- Location
- Type of property
- Size of property
- Condition of property
- Whether the property is vacant or tenanted

Location

When it comes to price, location is paramount. Prices vary wildly across different regions of the UK, with London and the South-East being more expensive than the North. For instance, between January 2012 and January 2013, house prices in London increased by 7.1%, whilst in the North-West of England they fell by 4.2% (www.landregistry.gov.uk).

There are also significant price differences within each region, each city, each town, and sometimes even each street, which are all to do with whether a location is popular. There are a number of things that cause an area to become unpopular including:

- High local unemployment
- High proportion of social housing
- Poor transport links
- Long distance to good schools
- High flood risk or a history of flooding
- Undesirable local features, e.g. sewage works
- Undesirable planned developments, especially infrastructure, e.g. a motorway close enough to produce excess noise
- High proportion of unoccupied properties and boarded up shops
- High local crime
- Proximity to flight paths for local airport

If your house price is affected by any of these things, there is little you can do about it, but the chances are that when you bought the house you benefitted from the low price of property in your area. The real sting comes when your area has deteriorated since you bought your house, or when developments since you bought have decreased your property's value.

On the other hand, you may have been fortunate enough to acquire a house in an area that might be described by estate agents as 'up and coming', perhaps an inner-city location that is undergoing regeneration.

'When it comes to price, location is paramount.'

When your house is valued, the estate agent will take all these things into consideration, with a house in the most sought-after part of town being offered at significantly more than an almost identical house in a less popular location.

Type of property

The price you can ask for your property will be affected by its type.

On the whole, you can ask more for bungalows than houses, as they occupy more land for the same internal area in square metres. Detached houses and bungalows are usually at the top of the price range within each area as the privacy afforded by this kind of housing is greatly prized.

A link-detached house, (one that does not share a party wall, but which is attached to its neighbour in some other way, usually by a garage) commands a slightly lower price than a detached, but slightly higher than a semi-detached.

A terraced house is usually valued at less than a semi-detached house. The properties on either end of the terrace are known as end-terraced houses, and are usually slightly higher in price than a mid-terraced house.

A flat or a maisonette is usually cheaper than a comparable house because many flats can occupy the same piece of ground. Land suitable for building on is expensive, and building upwards maximises the number of dwellings that can be fitted in.

Property size

Logically, you might assume that the larger the property, the higher the price you can ask for it. This is true – but only if all other factors, such as location and condition are equal.

Gardens and other land will increase the amount you can ask for your house, but if they are poorly maintained it will discourage buyers, who may see the mess and conclude that managing the land will be too much work.

Condition of property

The condition of your house is at least as important to its market price as size.

When buyers view your house, they are calculating how much money they will have to spend on it after they have bought it, to bring it to the condition they want. The more work that has to be done, the lower the price they will be prepared to offer.

How tenants affect sale value

Even the best tenants in the world will affect the sale value of your house, but it is all a question of degree.

If your house has long-term tenants who took on their tenancy before 15th January 1989, then its value will be seriously affected. Under this kind of tenancy, known variously as a protected tenancy, a regulated tenancy, or a sitting tenancy, the tenants cannot be evicted, except for failure to pay the rent on time, antisocial behaviour, or damage to the property. Furthermore, the tenants can apply for a 'fair rent', a sum which is nowhere near a market rent, and which is not decided by the landlord.

Not only will sitting tenants slash the value of your house by around 25%, but you may struggle to find a buyer at all.

If your tenants began their tenancy after 15th January 1989, the chances are that they have an Assured Shorthold Tenancy. This type of agreement allows the landlord to evict the tenants much more easily, giving two months' notice (as long as the first six months of the tenancy has been completed). This means that the house's sale value will hardly be affected at all.

However, having even this type of tenant in the property will affect the ease with which viewings can be conducted, and the tenants may not keep the house in the best condition to attract a buyer. It is not unheard of for a tenant who wishes to continue living in a property to make it so difficult to arrange viewings that the buyer gives up. It usually makes more sense for you to make sure the property is vacant before you put it on the market.

'The condition of your house is at least as important to its market price as size.'

Setting a sale price

The question of valuations is altogether simpler for a seller than a buyer. A buyer may need to consider the requirements of a lender, who will probably insist on a qualified chartered surveyor being used, preferably one who is a member of The Royal Institute of Chartered Surveyors. However, as a seller you can choose if you want this expensive service, or if you are satisfied with an assessment of value from someone who has fewer formal qualifications but is just as capable of helping you wisely pitch the sale price.

If you are using estate agents, they will advise on price. It is worth asking two or three agents to come and see your property. They may discuss whether you are in a hurry to sell the property (pushing the suggested sale price down), whether you have negative equity (keeping the sale price artificially high), and what price you expect to achieve.

If you are selling by auction, the auctioneer will advise you on sale value.

'The question of valuations is altogether simpler for a seller than a buyer.'

If you choose to sell by another method, you will need to obtain an independent valuation. Some estate agents are qualified to do this and will usually charge a fixed fee. Otherwise you will have few options other than using a chartered surveyor.

Sale price adjustments

Buyers expect to negotiate, especially in a buyer's market. You will probably want to put your house on the market at a few thousand more than the figure for which you are aiming. Then, during negotiations, you can drop the price somewhat without failing to meet your sale target.

A buyer who receives an unfavourable surveyor's report may wish to lower the original offer price, so consider whether you think a surveyor is likely to find a serious problem and decide whether to deal with it before marketing the house.

How stamp duty affects setting a sale price

Stamp duty land tax, known as 'stamp duty', is a tax that a buyer has to pay when a property is purchased. As this is something the buyer has to deal with, you may not think it affects you as a seller, but the existence of stamp duty has a bearing on the sale price.

Properties costing £125,000 or less are not liable for any stamp duty at all. If you price your house at £126,000, you will find that buyers are put off because they know that they will have to pay stamp duty.

Stamp duty is charged as a percentage of the entire sale price, and the percentage rises at certain thresholds. There are several other prices that will be tricky in this respect.

Stamp duty thresholds

Sale price	Stamp duty rate
Up to £125,000	0%
£125,000.01 - £250,000	1%
£250,000.01 - £500,000	3%
£500,000.01 - £1,000,000	4%
£1,000,000.01 - £2,000,000	5%
£2,000,000.01 upwards	7%

If you are thinking of pricing your house at just over the thresholds of a quarter of a million, half a million, one and two million, think again. Once the price has crossed the threshold, the applicable level of stamp duty is payable on *the whole price*. A buyer paying £250,000 will have to pay £2,500 stamp duty. A buyer paying £250,000.01, just one penny more, will be liable for £7,500 – three times as much.

How online property portals affect setting a sale price

When a house is advertised for sale online, buyers can browse properties by price. Websites such as Rightmove, PrimeLocation and Zoopla offer buyers a click list of minimum and maximum prices (see the help list). If, for example, your house is worth around a quarter of a million pounds, you may think it is a good move to price it at £249,999, hoping to make it look a lot less than a quarter of a million, and creeping in under the 3% stamp duty threshold. However, at this price it will not be selected by buyers who choose a range of £250,000-300,000. If you price it at over £250,000.01, the stamp duty will deter buyers. Despite all those fearsome noughts, it seems that £250,000 may be the best price after all.

Gazundering and gazumping

What is gazundering?

Once the price is agreed, you might be tempted to heave a huge sigh of relief and start calculating your profits. This may be premature, as you may yet become a victim of a gazunderer.

Gazundering is when a buyer demands a last-minute reduction in the price agreed. They may have sound reasons for doing so: perhaps a very slow transaction means that property prices have dropped significantly since the offer was accepted, or maybe the survey has pinpointed a problem.

However, it can just be the buyer simply grabbing an opportunity to get a better deal. If this is the case, the demand is likely to be timed carefully, at a point in the conveyancing process where you feel you have gone past the point of no return. After all, if the sale is cancelled just before exchange of contracts, you will have incurred quite a hefty amount of legal fees, which will still have to be paid. You will have to cancel your removal company and face starting to market your house all over again. If you are in a chain and you don't agree to the price reduction, the whole chain will collapse, including any purchase of your own.

'Gazundering is when a buyer demands a last-minute reduction in the price agreed.'

Need2Know

If you are selling in Scotland you are less likely to encounter this problem because of the differences in the conveyancing process. Any changes in sale price have to take place much earlier in the process.

What is gazumping?

The opposite of gazundering is gazumping, where the seller accepts a higher offer from another buyer. This leaves the original buyer out of pocket on legal expenses and survey fees, as well as wrecking a chain just as surely as gazundering does. Estate agents have a legal duty to inform sellers of offers, even after an offer has been accepted, and a seller can be tempted with a higher offer.

Both of these practices are ethically questionable, indeed in Scotland a solicitor will refuse to act for a seller who attempts to participate in gazumping, as, under the Law Society of Scotland code of practice, they would be guilty of misconduct if they continued to do so.

How can I avoid being gazundered?

Gazundering occurs more frequently in a buyer's market, and there is little you can do to protect against it, other than to ensure the conveyancing is done as quickly as possible before the value of your house drops. Up to exchange of contracts you will always be vulnerable.

A buyer can protect against being gazumped more easily than a seller can protect against being gazundered, as some insurance companies offer policies to cover gazumping. A buyer might also insist on an exclusivity agreement as part of their offer: this is where you, as seller, would have to sign an agreement not to accept an offer from any other buyer for a specified period of time.

Summing Up

- No house has a fixed, absolute value.

- The sale value of a property consists of the amount a buyer is willing to pay and a seller is willing to accept.

- The five main factors that affect the sale value of your house are its location, size, type and condition, and whether or not it is tenanted.

- Prices vary across the different regions of the UK, and also within each region, town or city. They also fluctuate according to whether it is a buyer's or a seller's market.

- A long-term tenancy that started before 15th January, 1989, will significantly lower the value of your property.

- Stamp duty thresholds and the constraints of online property portals may cause you to make small adjustments to your asking price, in order to attract the maximum number of buyers.

- Gazundering is when a buyer demands a last-minute reduction in price. Gazumping is when you accept a higher offer from a second buyer, after you have already agreed a price with the first buyer.

Chapter Three

Selling Through an Estate Agent

The property website Zoopla.co.uk says that 99% of sales are conducted through an estate agent. On the other hand, the Office of Fair Trading quotes figures showing that 10% of sellers sell privately. Whichever set of figures you choose to believe, it is still clear that estate agents are the most frequently used method of selling a house.

Why do most people sell through an estate agent?

The main purpose of an estate agent is to introduce buyers to sellers. There are a number of advantages to selling via an estate agent.

- Most buyers search for properties through estate agents, and many do not look elsewhere.

- Buyers can register with estate agents, who take a note of what type of property they are looking for and the price bracket they are prepared to consider. When you register your house for sale with an agent, the agent will match it to the waiting buyers. If you are lucky, this will generate a flurry of immediate viewings. You will occasionally see an estate agent advertising that they have sold a particular property within 24 hours, and this is how they do it.

- Estate agents can advertise on the main online property portals, but private individuals cannot. Nowadays, around 82% of property sales begin online and this figure is increasing

Who pays the estate agent?

The seller pays the estate agent, and the agent works for the seller, not the buyer. The service is free to the buyer. Agents charge the seller a percentage of the sale price, payable upon completion of the sale. The amount charged can range from as little as 0.5% plus VAT to around 3.5% plus VAT. According to a survey by *Which*, the average fee is 1.8% plus VAT.

How do I choose an estate agent?

It is common for a seller to appoint an agent on the basis of their fee, or because they have assigned a high valuation to the property to be sold. Neither of these is good reasons for selecting an agent.

'A lower estate agent fee does not necessarily equal a worse service, and a more expensive fee does not guarantee a better service.'

If you ask three agents to value your house and simply select the agent offering the highest valuation, you may be setting yourself up for disappointment. Because unwary sellers often do choose the agent who gives the highest valuation, an unscrupulous agent may suggest you can sell your house for an unrealistically high figure. When your house fails to sell at this price, they will suggest you reduce it, and you may end up with your house on the market for longer than if you had chosen a better agent.

A lower estate agent fee does not necessarily equal a worse service, and a more expensive fee does not guarantee a better service. However, it is undoubtedly true that some agents are better than others, and the best way to find this out is by reputation.

Useful questions to ask an estate agent include:

- Have you sold any properties in this road/immediate area recently?
- How long did it take to sell them?
- Did they achieve the asking price?
- What is the average time it takes your agency to sell a property?
- What services do the fees include?
- How often will my house be advertised in local papers, and will there be an additional fee for this?

- Which online property portals do you use for advertising?

- In the event of more than one buyer making an offer on my property, are you able to offer a sealed bid service?

- Is your agency a member of the National Association of Estate Agents?

- Is your agency a member of The Property Ombudsman or Ombudsman Services: Property?

These last two questions need a little more explanation.

The National Association of Estate Agents

This is a trade group of which membership is voluntary and means the agent agrees to abide by a certain set of standards. There is also no obligation for an estate agent to belong to the Royal Institute of Chartered Surveyors.

The Property Ombudsman and the Ombudsman Services: Property

These are two schemes approved by the Office of Fair Trading that provide redress in the event of a complaint by sellers or buyers against a registered agency. Your chosen agent should be a member of one of these schemes. Complaints about agencies that do not belong to either of these schemes can be made to the Office of Fair Trading.

The unfortunate fact is that there are no examinations to pass to become an estate agent. Your solicitor, who has had to study extensively and pass many exams, will typically earn much less from your house sale than your estate agent, who has likely done neither.

If you are still unsure about which estate agent to use, the National Association of Estate Agents offers a referral service.

What are the basic services offered by an estate agent?

Most agents include the following services in their fee:

- **Preliminary valuation** – Estate agents are experts on local prices. If you are thinking of putting your house on the market, most agents will be happy to visit the property, walk round it and suggest the kind of price they think it will fetch. There is usually no charge for this service (although it is wise to check this beforehand), and no obligation to use the agent. Unless the agent is also a chartered surveyor, the figure they give you is just an estimate of what they think your property will fetch when sold and has no official basis in law.

Some estate agents are members of the Royal Institute of Chartered Surveyors, and this mean they are able to do an official valuation (for tax purposes, for instance). You will be charged for an official valuation.

Asking two or three estate agents to visit your house is an excellent opportunity to see which one you feel most comfortable with, as well as a chance to ask them about the services they provide.

You do not have to market your property at the value estimated by an estate agent. If you wish, you can market it at the price you choose, and some people do this. However, these properties are often slow to sell, or do not sell at all, because they are overpriced in comparison with similar properties in the area. It is best to rely on the agent's expertise in this matter.

- **Advising on obstacles to selling** – If the agent suggests improvements you should make to your house, it is wise to take note. This advice is free, and comes from someone who is an expert in what attracts and deters buyers.

- **Advertising** – For the basic fee, you can expect the agent to visit your home to measure the rooms and take photographs, write a description of the property, and prepare a floor plan. This information is then put together in a document known as the 'sales particulars' which are used in advertising.

'Unless the agent is also a chartered surveyor, the figure they give you is just an estimate of what they think your property will fetch when sold and has no official basis in law.'

- **Introducing buyers to sellers** – When a buyer approaches an estate agent to view a house, the agent will normally contact the seller to arrange a viewing. Do not expect the agent to reveal the buyer's contact details. If you sell your house to a friend or personal contact who has not been introduced via the agent, you may still be liable to pay the estate agent's fee, unless the terms of your contract specifically allow for this.

- **Conducting viewings** – If your house is unoccupied, or if you are not available for viewings, you may prefer the agent to show buyers around your house on your behalf. This is a standard service that you do not have to use.

- **Negotiating** – The issue of agreeing a price is a tricky one, and most people in the UK are unused to negotiating prices for things they buy or sell. Some people feel embarrassed or intimidated by the process of haggling. Once a buyer has expressed an interest in buying the property, you should expect the agent to try to negotiate the best possible price, at the same time as trying not to lose the sale. However, beware an agent who pushes you to accept an offer with which you are not happy. Agents only make their money when a sale occurs, and your agent may prefer you to accept a lower offer than none at all. Listen to the agent's advice, but do not allow yourself to be pushed into selling at a price that leaves you dissatisfied.

'Beware an agent who pushes you to accept an offer with which you are not happy.'

  If someone makes an offer on your house, the estate agent is legally obliged to notify you in writing, even if the offer is ridiculous. They will normally also ring you with the offer, and discuss with you what response you wish to make.

  If you are fortunate enough to have more than one buyer making an offer for your house, the estate agent is in a position to play off the buyers against each other to gain the best possible price. However, agents are bound by industry rules and regulations, and codes of conduct. An agent should never tell a buyer that another buyer has made a higher offer if this is not the case, and doing this would be grounds for complaint and investigation.

- **Liaising with other parties involved in the sale** – Once a sale price has been agreed, the estate agent will liaise with your solicitor, notifying them of the price agreed, the name and details of the buyer, and of the buyer's solicitor.

If you choose a good agency, once an offer has been accepted, they will help to keep the whole sale process moving, checking up and down the chain and chasing up solicitors or buyers who are dragging their feet. Sadly, where an estate agency is not a good one, this job can all too often fall to you or your solicitor.

▓ **Other services** – Some agents offer other services, e.g. legal, financial, surveys, tenant finding, tenancy managing, or others. There is usually an additional fee for these services. Do not allow an agency to pressurise you into accepting additional services that you do not want. They may tell you that the sale will go more smoothly if you use their solicitors rather than your own, but they are saying this because they will get a referral fee. There is no obligation for you to sign up for these additional services, and if the agency insists there is, you will be better off finding a different agency.

What information will be included in the sales particulars?

The sales particulars are usually made up of:

▓ Photographs of your property, possibly inside as well as outside.

▓ A brief introductory description of the property.

▓ A description of each room and what it contains, along with room measurements.

▓ A floor plan.

▓ Whether the property is freehold, or leasehold, and, if applicable, the length and cost of the lease.

▓ A description or photographs, of land and other buildings attached to the property.

▓ The asking price – This will either be in the form of a 'guide price', 'offers over', 'fixed price', 'OIRO' (offers in the region of), or 'POA' (price on application: meaning a buyer has to ask the agent how much the property will cost).

▓ Details of whether the property is tenanted or 'vacant upon possession'.

▓ Whether the property is chain-free.

- Mention of any parking associated with the property, or a garage.

- A description of the local area.

- An Energy Performance Certificate.

- A location map.

If you are not happy with the photographs or the details written by the agent, ask for them to be redone or changed. However, under The Property Misdescriptions Act 1991, an agent can be sued for misrepresentation if they make statements about the property that are misleading or untrue, and most agents know the standards they must meet and will stick to them scrupulously. This legislation also covers the omission of information that could cause the buyer to make a different decision, and covers the printed word, photographs, plans, and also information given verbally. A seller misrepresenting a property could also face legal action.

How will an agent advertise my property?

The Internet

Nowadays the most effective way of advertising property is undoubtedly the Internet. There are a handful of dedicated websites (called online property portals) which handle most of the advertising for the property industry, and at present the most popular are: Rightmove, Zoopla and PrimeLocation (see the help list). These are free for buyers to use, and can be accessed from anywhere in the world. This is particularly useful for buyers who are looking to relocate from a distance.

When you are choosing an agent, ask which online property portals they use for advertising. Avoid agents who do not use the main websites as they will not be able to give your house the best level of exposure.

Agents will use all kinds of other technology to alert buyers to their property. Traditional mailings, whilst still used, now take second place to property particulars being sent to buyers electronically.

'If you are not happy with the photographs or the details written by the agent, ask for them to be redone or changed.'

Newspapers and magazines

Many agents have too many properties to advertise them all in the local paper each week, and so they operate a rota. For a specialised property sale, for instance a smallholding, they may also advertise in the specialist press: magazines or periodicals read by the kind of people who might buy that type of property.

Local advertising

Your agent will offer to put up a 'For Sale' sign outside your house. This is a proven method of selling, and it is important not to ignore local buyers who may not have access to the Internet. If you decide to allow this, discuss with your agent how the sign will be fixed. If you don't want holes drilled in your masonry, this is the time to say so. Some sellers prefer to be more discreet and will not wish to have this service.

Finally, agents usually run their business from a shop, where they advertise properties for sale. This is the traditional, tried-and-tested approach to selling, and it still works.

Can I use more than one estate agent?

When you hire one estate agency to sell your house, that agency becomes the 'sole agent'. However, you will sometimes see a house displaying 'For Sale' boards from more than one agent.

There are two ways of hiring more than one agent. One is by hiring two agents to act as 'joint sole agents', and the other is by using 'multiple agents'.

Joint sole agency

Joint sole agency is when you hire two agencies to represent your property. The fee charged is slightly higher than for a sole agency, and the two agents split the fee when the property is sold, no matter which one did the selling. The danger here is that one or both of the agencies concerned may become complacent and fail to work hard at selling your house, because they will get their fee even if the other agent does the selling. This type of agency works best when your house is likely to appeal to specialist buyers, e.g. an equestrian property, a smallholding or retail premises.

Multiple agency

Multiple agency is where you hire more than one estate agency, but only the agency that actually achieves the sale is paid. This type of agency carries the highest fees, because there is a risk to the estate agents that they will have to carry the expenses of advertising your property without receiving any payment at all. Because the agencies are in competition with each other, they will all work very hard to make the sale, but pushy agents will want you to accept the buyer they have introduced, even if the offer is very low. The table on the next page summarises the differences between these three types of agency representation.

'Multiple agency is where you hire more than one estate agency, but only the agency that actually achieves the sale is paid.'

	Sole agent	**Joint sole agents**	**Multiple agents**
Fees	One agent earns 100% of the fees paid.	Higher fees than the sole agent. The two agents split the fee no matter which one sells the property.	The highest fees of all. The agent that sells the property takes the whole fee.
When to use	Best in a seller's market, when there are fewer properties and more buyers.	Best when you want to use a general local agent plus a specialist national agent.	Best in a buyer's market, when there is a glut of properties and few buyers.
Advantages	The cheapest option.	Exposure to both local and specialist buyers.	Agents compete with each other to sell your property and be paid for free.
Disadvantages	Less exposure to buyers. May take longer to sell.	Agents may sit back and expect the other to do the work, as they will both get paid anyway.	Agents may try to pressurise you into accepting a lower offer rather than risk another agent getting the sale.

Estate agent's contract

What is likely to be in the estate agent's contract?

The clauses in the contract vary from one agency to another, but at the very least, your contract should mention:

- The type of representation (sole agency, joint sole agency or multiple agency).
- The length of the agreement.
- The details of how you can end the agreement.
- The amount of commission charged.
- Any other charges.
- The method of payment.
- Any services that may be offered to buyers.

What to do before you sign a contract with an estate agent

- Read the contract very carefully, including all the small print. Don't be embarrassed to take as much time as you need to do this properly
- Ask for clarification if there is anything you don't understand. Make sure everything is clear before you sign
- Check if there is a time limit on the contract. If you sign a sole agency contract with no time limit, and your estate agent turns out to be no good, it will be very difficult for you to obtain release from the contract and seek alternative representation elsewhere.
- Ask about the circumstances under which you can seek a release from the contract. How much notice do you have to give? Will there be a fee if you wish to terminate the contract?
- Will the agency allow joint sole agency or multiple agency? Some agents will only accept sole agency. If you sign a sole agency contract, will there be a possibility of changing it to a joint sole agency later on?

■ Can the rate be reduced? It is always worth asking

Summing Up

※ The majority of sales are conducted through an estate agent.

※ The estate agent works for, and is paid by, the seller. The average fee is 1.8% of the sale price plus VAT.

※ Avoid choosing an estate agent based solely on their fee or the value they assign your property. Instead, ask plenty of questions about how they operate and ask around locally to gauge their reputation.

※ The basic services offered by an estate agent are: preliminary valuation, advice on selling, advertising, introducing buyers, conducting viewings, negotiating a price, and liaising with other parties involved in the sale.

※ You may use more than one estate agent at the same time, but the terms and conditions, and the fees, will be different to a sole agency.

※ Read and check the contract very carefully before you sign it.

Chapter Four

Selling Through
an Auction

Selling through an auction is an unusual route for a private seller to take, with less than 25% of private property being sold in this way. However, certain types of property can do well at auction. These include:

- Houses requiring extensive modernisation or renovation.

- Commercial premises or investment properties (i.e. properties that produce an income).

- Land.

- Development properties.

- Properties that are difficult to sell through an agent.

- Houses that have been on the open market for a long time.

- Properties on which it is difficult to get a mortgage.

- Unusual or novelty properties which are difficult to value.

Although private sellers do not tend to use auctions, there is nothing stopping them from doing so. Over recent years, television has popularised the idea of finding bargain properties at auctions, and there is a gradual creep towards private individuals using this method of buying and selling properties.

What does it cost to sell through an auction?

Like an estate agent, an auction house will charge a fee which is a percentage of the selling price of your house. This is typically 2.5%, although it varies from one auction house to another.

In addition to this fee, there will be other costs, depending on which auction house you choose. At the very least, these may include fees for photographs, advertising costs, and inclusion in brochures and catalogues.

It is important to remember that you will have to pay these additional costs even if your house fails to sell at the auction. This is in contrast with the system used by estate agents, where there is usually a no-sale, no-fee arrangement.

Before signing any agreement, make sure you are clear about the costs involved, including those you will have to pay even if your house is not sold at the auction. Read the contract carefully and ask for anything you do not understand to be explained.

'Like an estate agent, an auction house will charge a fee which is a percentage of the selling price of your house.'

Taking all this into account, it will usually be more expensive for you to sell your house at auction than through an agent. So why do people use this method?

Advantages of selling through an auction

- It is often faster than selling through an estate agent. Generally, the process takes about 8 to 10 weeks and the sale is usually completed within 28 days (or 20 working days) after the auction.

- When the hammer falls, the buyer is legally bound to proceed with the sale. A buyer who does not complete the sale will forfeit the deposit and face other heavy penalties, which can include paying the difference between the price agreed and the price for which you finally sell your house. Therefore, it is extremely unlikely that a buyer will pull out at the last minute.

- The seller does not get involved in a house-buying chain.

- In the case of a desirable property, it is possible that a bidding frenzy may push the price above that which would have been achieved if it had been marketed through an agent.

Disadvantages of selling through an auction

- It is common for properties to be sold for a lower price than if sold through an agent, although this is not always the case.

- You are limited to a smaller number of potential buyers, because buyers requiring a mortgage do not usually purchase at auctions.

- Selling at auction can be more expensive than selling through an estate agent. If your house is not sold, there will still be charges to pay.

How does the process differ from selling through an estate agent?

The same legal procedures have to be gone through, regardless of whether the property is sold through auction or through an agent. The differences lie in the timing and who does what and when.

The chart on the next page shows the differences in the order in which things take place when selling through an auction. The most significant difference is that the buyer has a chance to fully investigate the legal documents *before* any offer is made. This is because the seller's solicitor produces a legal pack that is made available to buyers before the auction. A cautious and sensible buyer will also have a survey conducted on the property before the auction.

When selling through an estate agent, all the information in the auction pack has to be investigated *after* the offer has been accepted, and this is also when the survey is done. It is at this stage that a buyer may find out something that makes the property undesirable, e.g. a right of way, an access issue, or a serious fault with the property, such as subsidence.

In other words, when selling through an agent, uncertainty remains about whether the sale will go through, right up to a couple of days before the property changes hands and the keys are handed over. On the other hand, when selling through an auction, once the hammer falls, the sale is practically guaranteed, giving the seller not only peace of mind, but financial compensation if the sale then fails.

'The same legal procedures have to be gone through, regardless of whether the property is sold through auction or through an agent.'

This difference in the order that things are done means that searches have to be done by the seller, for the benefit of all the potential buyers, rather than by the eventual buyer.

The buyer becomes responsible for the insurance on the house at the fall of the auctioneer's hammer, rather than upon completion of the sale.

Selling at auction	Selling through an estate agent
The sale preparation stage	**The sale preparation stage**
The seller appoints an auctioneer.	The seller appoints an estate agent.
The seller appoints a solicitor.	The seller appoints a solicitor.
The auctioneer visits the house to value it and obtain information for marketing purposes.	The estate agent visits the house to value it and obtain information for marketing purposes.
The seller agrees a guide price with the auctioneer.	The seller agrees a marketing price with the estate agent.
The auctioneer advertises the house.	The estate agent advertises the house and arranges viewings.
	A buyer makes an offer on the house and, usually after negotiations, a price is agreed upon.
The legal stage	**The legal stage**
The seller's solicitor prepares contracts and a legal pack, including searches. Searches are paid for by the seller.	The buyer will usually arrange for a survey at this point.
The seller agrees a reserve price with the auctioneer, based upon the interest at the viewings and the kinds of buyers who are interested.	The buyer's solicitor conducts searches. Searches are paid for by the buyer.
The auctioneer makes the legal pack available to buyers and arranges a viewing day or days.	The seller's solicitor provides other legal documents.
Prospective buyers may conduct surveys upon the building.	The seller's solicitor prepares contracts.

The sale	**The sale**
The auction takes place. The buyer makes a successful bid for the house.	When all the paperwork is in place, exchange of contracts takes place. *At this point the buyer is legally bound to complete the sale.*
The buyer signs the contract in the auction room and pays a deposit of 10%. This is equivalent to exchange of contracts if selling through an agent. *At this point the buyer is legally bound to complete the sale.*	The sale is completed, usually within two or three days.
The buyer becomes responsible for insurance on the house when the contract is signed.	The seller vacates the house and hands over the keys at completion of the sale.
The sale is completed within 28 days.	
The seller vacates the house and hands over the keys at completion of the sale.	

Choosing an auction house

If you decide to sell your house through an auction, select your auction house carefully. You will need to look for an auction house that deals in the type of property you are trying to sell. A company that deals mainly with farms and agricultural land is unlikely to get the best price for your London flat.

There are two main types of auction house: local and national.

National auction houses

A company that operates right across the UK is likely to be best placed to sell unusual properties with novelty value, so this is probably the best type to select if you are selling a converted windmill or a chapel that has been turned into a home. Such a company is likely to hold auctions in London or another big centre, where properties from right across the UK are sold.

Local auction houses

A local auction house, which often doubles as an estate agency, will have the contacts and expertise to market the type of property that is likely to appeal to local buyers, as well as having the edge on setting a price that accurately reflects house values in your area. A small terraced house in North Yorkshire is not likely to attract huge interest at an auction held in London, nor will buyers of inexpensive properties wish to travel so far to attend the auction. With around 200 auction houses in the UK that sell homes, there is likely to be one in your area.

If you can find an auction house that operates both nationally and locally, you will get the best of both worlds, with advertising on a national scale and a local auction. However, with the advent of Internet property portals, national exposure is now much easier to achieve with a local auctioneer than it used to be.

'The reserve price is the lowest price the seller is willing to accept. It is not necessarily the same amount as the guide price, although it can be.'

The guide price and the reserve price

The guide price is agreed between the seller and the auctioneer, and will form part of the advertising for the property. The guide price tells buyers roughly what price the property is expected to sell for. Setting the guide price is a delicate issue: it has to be low enough to attract bidders to the auction, but not so low that they feel cheated by the selling price rising way above the guide price.

The reserve price is the lowest price the seller is willing to accept. It is not necessarily the same amount as the guide price, although it can be. If the highest bid received during the auction is lower than the reserve price, then the property will not be sold. The reserve price is agreed privately between the seller and the auctioneer and is not a piece of information that is available to buyers or any other member of the public.

What happens if my house doesn't reach the reserve price?

If your house fails to sell during the auction because the highest bid is below the reserve price, all is not necessarily lost. The auctioneer will announce that the house is not sold, and will invite anybody still interested in buying to talk to a member of staff after the auction. Quite a number of properties are sold in this way, although buyers tend to take advantage of the failed auction sale to offer as low a price as possible. They know that you, as the seller, will still have bills to meet, even though your house has not sold, and they will be hoping that you will accept a lower offer.

You do not need to get personally involved in these discussions: auctioneers are experienced at representing their clients in negotiations.

Some auction houses retain your property on their books for as much as a month after the auction (the terms and conditions you agree with them at the beginning will give you information on this) and, if the property is sold during this period, the terms and conditions of the sale will be the same as if you had sold in the auction room on the day of sale.

What happens if someone makes an offer for my house before the auction?

From time to time, a buyer will try to buy an auction property before the date of the sale. This is quite normal, and many sales are agreed in this way, with the house simply being withdrawn from the auction.

The advantage to you, as the seller, means that you have achieved a sale. The disadvantage is that you may accept an offer that might have been surpassed during the bidding at the sale.

Should I attend the sale?

There is no obligation on you, as the seller, to attend the auction. Your presence is not required, although some auctioneers will ask you to make sure your solicitor attends to answer any last-minute questions. Check with the auctioneer to see if this is required, as a solicitor's time is very expensive and you will be the one picking up the bill.

Although you do not need to be at the sale, it can be interesting and exciting, especially if the bidding is brisk and the price begins to rise above the reserve.

How the auctioneer can help you achieve the best price

An auction house with local knowledge will be invaluable in setting an enticing, but realistic guide price. Of course, this type of expertise can also be obtained from a local estate agent. But once the buyers are at the sale, auctioneers often have a few other tricks up their sleeve.

Once the bidding begins the sale tends to gather momentum with the bidders becoming competitive, so getting that first bid is vital. It is not unknown for the auctioneer to take a bid from thin air, giving everyone the impression that someone has started the bidding when, in fact, nobody has begun to bid!

The auctioneer knows what buttons to press to keep buyers bidding, and when it seems as if no more bids are forthcoming, they will indicate to the bidders that the hammer is about to be brought down. This often prompts buyers to make one more bid, and the sale continues.

Incredible though it seems, it is perfectly legal for the auctioneer to bid on behalf of the seller. As long as the bid is below the reserve price, the house will not be sold, and this helps to push up the price if there is only one bidder.

The auctioneer will also accept bids by telephone. This method is used when a buyer cannot attend a sale, but wishes to bid. A member of staff of the auction house will remain in telephone contact with the bidder during the sale, and will bid on their behalf as they instruct.

When the hammer falls, no more bids can be taken.

After the sale

If your house has reached its reserve price, then you can breathe a sigh of relief when the hammer falls. In theory, all you have to do now is sit back, wait for time to pass, and ensure you vacate the property and finalise the utility bills by the 28th day. This is in stark contrast to when you sell by private treaty, where the deal can fall through right up to the last minute.

Having said that, there are rare occasions when the buyer fails to complete a sale made at auction. The only consolation for the time, trouble and money that this will cost you is that the buyer will face severe penalties and will have to reimburse you financially. Sadly, there is no type of house sale that is completely certain, although selling by auction comes close.

'Sadly, there is no type of house sale that is completely certain, although selling by auction comes close.'

Summing Up

- Certain types of property do better than others when sold through auction.

- It is generally slightly more expensive to sell a house at auction than through an estate agent. In addition, there will be costs to pay even if your house does not sell.

- As well as being a fast method of selling, an auction gives you more certainty that the sale will go through.

- The price you achieve may be lower than if you sell by another method, although an unusual or sought-after property may do particularly well.

- The same legal procedures have to be gone through, regardless of whether the property is sold through auction or through an agent. The differences lie in the timing and who does what and when.

- Choose an auction house that normally deals with the type of property you are trying to sell.

- Your house may be sold before the auction, or even afterwards in some cases.

- You do not have to attend the sale if you do not wish to do so.

- You must vacate your house within 28 days of a successful sale.

Chapter Five

Selling Privately

Why sell privately?

There is a growing trend for individuals to cut out the estate agent and sell their homes privately. In the past this was difficult, but nowadays the Internet makes it easier.

People choose to sell privately for a variety of reasons:

- Dissatisfaction with the service they have received in the past from estate agents.
- The high cost of selling through high street estate agents or auction houses.
- The ease and cost of advertising online.
- A desire to be in full control of the selling process.

It is not a legal requirement to use an estate agent, nor does it necessarily guarantee a faster sale or a higher selling price. There are other ways to find buyers.

You can choose to sell privately without using the Internet, by simply erecting a 'For Sale' notice outside your house and putting an advert in the local paper. However, most buyers now begin their search for a home online, so the low-tech approach is less likely to result in a successful sale.

'It is not a legal requirement to use an estate agent, nor does it necessarily guarantee a faster sale or a higher selling price.'

Where should I start?

Begin in the same way as you would for a sale by any other method: prepare your house and decide on the price you want to ask for it. You will still need a solicitor, just as with a sale by more traditional methods, so engage one before you begin. Tell your solicitor that you are planning a private sale.

Next, you must decide which method of selling privately you want to use. These are:

■ Through an online estate agent

■ Through a private sales website

■ Through another kind of advertising website, e.g. eBay

■ By advertising locally

Selling through an online estate agent

Online estate agents are governed by the same regulations as high street estate agents and have to comply with the 1979 Estate Agency Act. Most online estate agents have a fixed fee for using their services, usually with part or all of it payable upfront. Whilst it is true that this cost will still be incurred if you fail to sell your house, it is potentially thousands of pounds cheaper than high street estate agent fees. Online agents can keep their fees low because they do not have the overheads of running high street shops.

When choosing online estate agents, the minimum requirements should be:

■ They are a member of the National Association of Estate Agents and an Ombudsman scheme.

■ They will visit your home and take photographs and measurements.

■ They will produce a floor plan.

■ They will provide a 'For Sale' board.

■ They will advertise your property on all of the most popular property portals.

■ They will liaise with buyers on your behalf, including initial enquiries, sending out details, arranging viewings, giving feedback and negotiating price.

- They should advertise your property until it is sold with no additional fees or hidden extra costs.

Optional services that some online agents provide are:

- A dedicated website for your property

- A virtual tour

- Advertising in local newspapers

- Conducting viewings

Selling through a private sales website

This type of website allows you to advertise your house without using an agent. There are two crucial differences between these sites and online estate agents:

- Advertising is the only service provided, so you will have to do all the tasks that are normally done by the agent.

- Your property will not be advertised on the popular online property portals like Rightmove, Zoopla and PrimeLocation. These sites only accept property being sold through agents.

Some popular websites for private house sales are:

- PropertyBroker

- Tepilo

- NoEstateAgentsPlease.com

- HouseWeb

The most useful website you can visit if you want to take a look at private sales websites is www.sellersnet.co.uk. This site brings together and provides links to most of the relevant websites, and subdivides them into online estate agents, private property listings and classified ads. It is an ideal website to browse to help you compare and choose which sites to use.

The main disadvantage of selling by this method is the relatively small number of buyers who browse such websites. The private advertising sites have only a small number of properties compared with the major property portals, and the buyers that do search the private advertising websites are therefore less likely to find a property in which they are interested. Also, anyone used to searching on Rightmove, Zoopla and PrimeLocation may find the search methods on some of these sites unfamiliar and not always user-friendly.

Selling on eBay

A buyer browsing eBay for property has to overcome a number of hurdles.

To begin with, they must register with eBay and bid through the website for any property they want to buy.

There is also the problem of finding properties to view. As an example, today I entered 'house for sale', which brought up 370 items. This seemed promising, but only 3 of these properties were in London, the target of my search, and the items listed also, inexplicably, included a Royal Doulton figurine and a wide selection of labels. 'Property for sale' yielded 212 items, some of which were toys or models. (This is a good search to make if you want to buy a 'For Sale' sign, as a number of these also came up.) 'Flat for sale' gave me 151 items including flat screen TVs, flat shoes and flat tyres!

Of course, it *is* possible to sell a house on eBay, and some people do so. However, it will be an uphill struggle for your buyer, who will be used to the clean and targeted property searches available on the main property portals, and who may be disinclined to wade through dozens of properties in Bulgaria or scores of flat shoes. You have to depend upon the buyer being lucky enough to enter a search that actually brings your property up onto their screen.

Other advertising websites suffer the same kind of problems, particularly if they are not selling exclusively property. Some are so user-unfriendly that they are virtually impossible to use. It is recommended that you try out websites as if you were a browsing buyer looking for a house in your area to see what kind of experience you have. If you cannot pinpoint the kind of property or the area you are looking for, the chances are that others will not be able to do so either.

Selling by advertising locally

Look in any local newspaper and you are likely to find estate agents advertising properties. Even in this digital age agents continue to advertise in local papers, partly because that is what sellers expect them to do, and partly because it is an important way of attracting new sellers. Now that the majority of buyers begin their search for a house online the efficacy of newspaper advertising is debateable. However, undoubtedly there are some sales that are achieved through newspaper advertisements.

Your advertisement is in danger of being overlooked unless it is large and includes a photograph. Remember to include a contact telephone number and the location of the property, not only the street, but the town. If this piece of advice seems so obvious as to be insulting, just look at your local paper to see how many properties are advertised as 'town centre' without actually mentioning which town! In papers which serve rural areas that include a number of small towns, this is especially important.

Remember that the law does not allow you to misrepresent your property. If you are writing the advertisement, getting the facts right is your responsibility alone.

If you are committed to the local selling route, remember that you can advertise on newsagents' advertising boards, or customer advertising displays at your local supermarket. These methods may not have the power of the Internet to be read by thousands, but you only need one buyer, and that person may be someone who shops locally.

> 'Now that the majority of buyers begin their search for a house online the efficacy of newspaper advertising is debateable.'

'For Sale' boards

Do not omit to place a 'For Sale' board outside your house. Sale boards are a proven selling tool, generating as many as a quarter of all sales enquiries. There are planning restrictions on the size and location of advertising boards, and these vary from one local authority to another, so check with your local authority planning office before you buy or erect a sign. Typically, a local authority may specify that the sign may have to be less than a certain size and not displayed above a certain height. If your house is a listed building or in a conservation area, there may be special restrictions about how the board can be fixed to the house, or indeed, whether it can be fixed to the building at all.

You can find companies that make signs on the Internet, or by looking in your local telephone book or business directory under 'Sign Makers'.

Getting organised

If you are selling privately you will have to devote a substantial amount of time to your sale, as you will be undertaking functions normally done by an estate agent. These include:

- Advertising (including photos and written descriptions)
- Organising a 'For Sale' board
- Fielding enquiries, sending out details, answering queries
- Arranging and conducting viewings
- Negotiating a price
- Chasing up other parties during the sale process

It is best to think about how you will do these things before you start.

It is wise to keep your weekends fairly free during the viewing stage. Saturday is the most popular day for viewing and you will lose buyers if you are unavailable. Similarly, it would be challenging to conduct your own sale successfully unless you have access to a telephone at all times, and are able to talk to buyers during your working hours. Buyers ring at all times of day, and will not necessarily limit themselves to evening calls.

As an optimistic seller, you need to have details ready to post and send by email to buyers. Keep a record of enquiries, and make follow-up calls to buyers to whom you have sent details. After viewings, always telephone to get feedback. Even if a buyer does not want your house, you can learn why from their comments, and you may be able to tweak your house presentation, your viewing technique or your advertising in the light of the feedback.

'It is wise to keep your weekends fairly free during the viewing stage. Saturday is the most popular day for viewing and you will lose buyers if you are unavailable.'

Selling privately as well as with an agent

An increasing number of sellers are using online advertising at the same time as a high street estate agent.

The important thing to remember, if you decide to do this, is that there are some very grey areas concerning commission. If you already have an estate agent, you should check carefully your contract. It is likely to say that you must pay the agency commission if unconditional contracts for the sale of the property are exchanged with a buyer introduced by the agency, or with whom they have negotiated about the property. The contract may also explain that a buyer may be introduced directly or indirectly by the agent, a clause allowing the agent to take credit for a sale when it may not truthfully be due.

All this makes it very difficult for a seller to prove that a buyer was introduced to the property as a result of the seller's, rather than the estate agent's activity. It may be that you end up with a buyer who saw your private advertisement, but who is also registered with your estate agent.

The best thing to do is to hammer out an agreement with the agent before you sign any contract with them, and make sure that the agreement forms part of the written contract. Should you be aware of interest in your property from specific friends or family, identify them to the agent and ask that a sale to them be excluded from the contract.

Read the contract carefully to make sure that it does not exclude private Internet advertising. If such a clause is in the contract, ask for it to be removed, or go to a different agency.

'Cash for property' buyers

There are many companies that advertise they will buy your property very quickly for cash. Some will claim that the money can be in your bank account within 7 days, or even 24 hours. Others will claim that they will pay 100% of the value of your house. Beware, as these claims are not always matched by reality.

This type of buyer operates as a business, and is not buying your house in order to live in it. They will be intending to sell your house on at a profit. This means they are really very unlikely to pay you 100% of the market value of the house. It is much more likely that they will pay you 100% of *their valuation* of your house, and some of these companies will charge you a hefty fee to make the valuation as well.

It would be most unusual for you to receive a market price for your house if you sell it in this way. The website theadvisory.co.uk says that most sales of this type that they have observed fetch 75-80% of the 'realistic value' (defined as the price that would achieve a sale in 6 weeks).

Only sell your house in this way if your need to sell is so urgent that you are prepared to accept a price well below market value. If your need is urgent, but you can wait a few weeks, consider using an auction house instead.

Sale and rent back

In 2008, The Office of Fair Trading investigated the sale-and-rent-back industry and the Financial Services Authority began regulating these businesses in 2009. By 2012, the sale-and-rent-back sector had almost completely closed down, as firms were unable or unwilling to comply with the regulation.

The Citizens Advice Bureau advises that this kind of scheme should only be considered as a last resort, when all other options have been exhausted. If you really must go down this route, before you enter into any agreement you should:

- Check if the company is listed on the Financial Services Register run by the Financial Conduct Authority. Go to www.fca.org.uk to do this. If the company is not listed, do not use it.

- Check the terms and conditions of the scheme extremely carefully. Remember you could still get evicted if you contravene the terms of your tenancy agreement or if the company that has bought your house goes into receivership.

- Check you are being offered a fair price. If you are being offered less than your outstanding mortgage, your lender can refuse to let you sell the house.

- Check that your entitlements to state benefits will not be affected.

Equity release

Equity release schemes are not the same as selling a house, but can sometimes be perceived as such. These schemes allow you to take cash as a loan, set against the equity you have built up in your property (i.e. the amount of your property that you have paid for). There are two types of scheme:

* Lifetime mortgages – These allow you to borrow a lump sum or an income set against your property, which you continue to own and live in. When you die or go into long-term care, the house is sold and the loan and the compound interest are paid back. This is a very expensive way of borrowing money.

* Home reversion schemes – These allow you to sell part or all of your property to the company and use the money, but still remain living in your house. When the house is sold, the company takes a percentage of the price corresponding to the percentage that it bought, and you get whatever remains.

If you are considering an equity release scheme, remember that it is not the same as selling your house. It is simply another way of borrowing money.

'Equity release schemes allow you to take cash as a loan, set against the equity you have built up in your property.'

Summing Up

- People choose to sell privately to save money and because they want to be in full control of the selling process.

- Begin by preparing your house, deciding on a price, instructing a solicitor and choosing which selling method you prefer.

- Online estate agents are regulated in the same way as high street estate agents, but charge less. Fees are usually payable up front, rather than after a sale.

- Online advertising is cheap, but not necessarily cost-effective, as you may not reach your target audience.

- Advertising locally without using the Internet is not recommended if you are looking for a quick sale, as most people begin their search for a house online.

- 'For Sale' boards are effective at generating interest in a house.

- If you want to use an estate agent and advertise privately as well, discuss this with the agent before you sign the contract and make sure whatever you agree is included in writing in the contract, otherwise you may end up paying the agent a fee even if they did not introduce the buyer.

- Only sell your house to a fast-buy company if your need to sell is so urgent that you are prepared to accept a price below market value.

- Equity release schemes are not about selling your house, but about borrowing money.

Chapter Six

Preparing Your House for the Sale

Once you have decided to put your house on the market, you will want to attract buyers and achieve the highest possible price. Even if you are short of funds and in a hurry, a moderate amount of strategic work can improve your chances of selling quickly at an advantageous price.

It is very difficult to look objectively at your home, but you have to do this in order to see what changes you can make to the property to make it more attractive. If you are really unsure of how to present your house, you could ask a friend, or your estate agent, to suggest changes you might make.

Consider the following questions, to see if any of them apply to your house.

Do I need to consider expensive renovations?

If you have the time, money and expertise to make alterations to your house, do so only with an eye to whether the work will increase its market value. The danger is that you might spend £10,000 on having work done on the house, only to discover that it increases the value of the house by only £5,000. Most standard housing has a 'ceiling price' in any particular area, an amount over which a buyer will look to a buy a similar property in a better area.

Consider the following example. A two-bedroomed house on Long Street will not normally sell for more than £120,000, because it is in a less sought-after part of town. A three-bedroomed house on the same street may have a ceiling of £135,000. You decide to do a loft conversion which provides an extra bedroom, but the cost comes in at £20,000. If you achieve the expected market price for your house, you will have lost £5,000 by having done the work.

'A moderate amount of strategic work can improve your chances of selling quickly at an advantageous price.'

If you are in any doubt, ask the advice of a local estate agent. When you ask for a valuation, take the opportunity to tell the agent about the kind of work you are thinking of doing, and check if it will increase the value of the property beyond the price of the work.

Will the layout deter buyers?

The main purpose of any renovations will be to make the property more attractive to buyers. This can sometimes mean changing its layout, as poor layout will deter buyers. For instance, in smaller houses a kitchen/diner is currently more fashionable than a separate small kitchen and small dining room. Can the two rooms be knocked into one? Long, dark corridors leading away from the front door used to be fashionable, but nowadays tend to put buyers off.

Never, never try to knock down a wall without first engaging a structural engineer to advise you. If you remove a supporting wall (i.e. a wall that is carrying the weight of the storeys above), you risk total disaster.

Is my house old-fashioned?

Trends come and go, and a house can start looking dated within ten or twenty years. Updating is a very worthwhile exercise and will not only add value to your property, but will make it more attractive to buyers.

Updating is often a matter of superficial work. There are certain patterns of wallpaper and carpets that evoke a not only a very specific decade, but also a strong negative reaction from buyers. It costs relatively little to renew carpets, but to great effect. Fashions in other types of floor coverings change over time, too. Linoleum is now considered old-fashioned, while wood and laminate floors are currently popular.

Nowadays, a home with no central heating will deter buyers, although this was perfectly acceptable thirty years ago. With fuel prices rocketing, insulation is becoming more and more important, and any deficiency in this area will be highlighted by your house's Energy Performance Certificate. Buyers may ask to see recent bills to assess how expensive it will be to run the house, so it is in your interest to make sure you have as much insulation as possible.

If your kitchen is shabby, a less expensive alternative to installing a new kitchen is to replace the cupboard doors. This will only work if the carcasses and draw units are still in reasonable condition.

Should I redecorate?

It is sometimes difficult to look past strong décor to see the potential of a house. If your teenage son has decorated his room with purple walls and a black ceiling, it is fair to say that buyers will probably be put off!

Whatever colour you select for redecoration, it is unlikely to suit everybody's taste, so try to choose pale, neutral, inoffensive tones, with a hint of warmth.

Is my house basically sound?

Unless you are prepared to adversely affect the asking price, you should ensure that the house is sound and in basic working order. In particular, buyers will be put off by expensive structural problems, such as a roof needing repair, untreated damp problems, and walls where the plaster is coming away.

It is this type of issue that so often stalls or kills a sale. When a buyer makes an offer 'subject to survey' and the surveyor reports that the house has serious damp, dry rot, or some other worrying basic fault, one of two things will happen. Either the buyer will consider the cost of the work needed and lower the offer price, or the defect will cause the whole sale to fall through.

Does everything in my house work as it should?

Go through the house, room by room, checking everything over. Look for visual defects, such as peeling wallpaper or limescale-encrusted taps, as well as mechanical problems, such as faulty locks or toilets that won't flush properly unless you pump the handle in a special way. These details may seem minor to you, but there are buyers out there who are very picky.

Repairs such as these are usually relatively cheap and easy to do. It is probably fair to say that buyers will not notice the work you have done, but they will almost certainly notice if you do not do it. In deciding between two similar houses, maintenance is something that can make or break a sale.

How can I make the rooms look bigger?

Banish clutter

If you are hoping to move to a larger property, the chances are that you and your family have outgrown your current home, and your house may be cluttered, giving the impression that the property is small and cramped. But where to put everything?

'Maintenance is something that can make or break a sale.'

One solution is to hire temporary storage and move into it items that are not often needed, such as Christmas decorations, books and ornaments. Moving house is also a great opportunity to have a sort out and get rid of things that are no longer required.

Maximise internal light

Nobody wants to live in a dark house. Also, the more light there is in a room, the larger it will seem. In an east-west facing house, the natural light is distributed fairly evenly throughout the rooms, but if your house is north-south facing, it is likely that the rooms on the north side are quite dark.

There are some simple ways to introduce light into rooms:

- Decorate in pale colours.
- Ensure ceilings are clean.
- Trim back trees, bushes and hedges that are close to windows.
- Hang a large mirror so that it reflects window light into the room.
- Keep windows clean.
- Use pale floor colourings and soft furnishings.

- Take down net curtains.
- Make sure all curtains and internal doors are fully open during viewings.

How can I maximise 'kerb appeal'?

'Kerb appeal' means the attractiveness of a property from the outside. Take a walk up your garden path and try to imagine you are looking at your house for the first time. Is the front garden full of weeds? Is there cat poo on the path? Does your hedge need trimming? Is the gate broken?

A shabby property will suggest to a buyer that money will need to be spent on it, and so any offer a buyer makes will take this expected expenditure into account. So take some time to paint the door, tidy up the front garden, and remove the weeds from the gutter.

To enable buyers to find your house easily, ensure the number or name of the house is clearly visible.

Should I 'dress up' an empty property?

This is called 'home staging', which means transforming an empty property into a living space where buyers can imagine themselves living, helping those buyers who find it difficult to imagine what an empty room will look like when it is furnished.

If your property is inexpensive, it may be sufficient to acquire some clean, second-hand furniture at an auction or from classified advertisements. If you do your own home staging, furniture bought for this purpose can be resold after a sale has been agreed.

For highly priced properties it may be worth paying a specialist home staging company, because good home staging can both increase the sale value of a property and help you achieve a faster sale.

Staging is about more than just furnishing a house. It is about mood, atmosphere, lifestyle and other similar intangibles. Home staging companies have a vast store of 'props' and aim to evoke an emotional reaction. They will use different fabrics, light angles and groups of furniture and props to great artistic effect, with the overall aim of creating a 'wow factor'.

Can I add value by extending my lease?

Because flats share the same piece of building land the type of tenure is not the same as a house.

There are two types of tenure, freehold and leasehold. Unless you buy a whole block of flats, you are likely to find a leasehold agreement attached to a flat.

If you own a property freehold, it means you also own the land upon which the building sits. A leasehold ownership, on the other hand, means that someone else owns the land, and leases it to you for the purpose of keeping your property on it.

'Do not overlook the possibility of adding value to your house by doing nothing more than a bit of paperwork.'

Leases are usually quite long, a hundred years or even several hundred years, and the lease is sold along with the property. Obviously the lease runs its course year by year, and the value of a property can be affected by the length of the lease remaining. A short lease, say twenty or thirty years, can significantly reduce the asking price. When leases become short, they are usually renegotiated at the point of sale, but buyers know that this means delays and increased legal fees.

If you have a leasehold property where the remaining period of lease is less than thirty or forty years, you can significantly increase the asking price by renegotiating the lease prior to putting the home on the market. It will take quite a long time to do this, as the lease will have to be simultaneously renegotiated for all flats affected by the lease, but if you have the time to spare it will usually be financially worth your while.

Does my house have 'potential to expand'?

Estate agents like to highlight if a house has 'potential to expand'. This can simply mean it has enough garden space for an extension, or an attic that could be converted. More temptingly, it can sometimes mean that planning permission has already been approved for work to be carried out.

Do not overlook the possibility of adding value to your house by doing nothing more than a bit of paperwork. If your house is advertised 'with planning permission for a two-storey extension', for instance, it will push up the price that buyers are willing to pay. It will not increase the price as much as the extension itself, but then planning permission is much, much cheaper for you than the cost of the extension.

Summing Up

- Only undertake large projects such as altering layout if the increase in the asking price justifies the cost of the work.

- Review your house objectively to see if it looks dated. Consider updating superficial or decorative features. If you redecorate, choose neutral, inoffensive colour schemes.

- Ensure that the house is sound and in basic working order, and attend to minor repairs. Check out how it looks from the outside.

- Make the rooms look bigger by clearing out clutter, cleaning and tidying, and maximising light.

- Consider home staging an empty property.

- If your lease is becoming short, think about negotiating a longer lease before you put the property on the market.

- If your house has potential to expand, consider if it is worth applying for planning permission.

Chapter Seven

Viewings

Should I ask the estate agent to conduct viewings for me?

You are the expert on your house, and you may relish the opportunity to show people around and give them a personal view of the property. However, if you are not confident about conducting viewings yourself, or if you are out a great deal, it is quite in order to ask your estate agent to do viewings for you. This is called 'accompanied viewing'. If your agent does not offer accompanied viewings, you can ask for this service, which should not cost you any extra. Indeed, many agents prefer to show prospective buyers around your house themselves, for the following reasons:

- They are expert at judging buyer interest.

- They are experienced at noticing what aspects of a house interest a buyer and directing their attention to these.

- They are accustomed to dealing with awkward questions.

- They know what *not* to say.

However, do not feel that you have to go down this route. Many people conduct viewings themselves when selling their properties.

'If your agent does not offer accompanied viewings, you can ask for this service, which should not cost you any extra.'

What should I do if someone knocks on the door and asks to look around?

For safety and security, always make appointments for viewings, rather than just showing round strangers who knock on the door. Do this even if you are selling your house privately and not using an estate agent. This way you have a name and a contact number, which will discourage opportunist thieves and those who want to check out if your home contains any valuables.

When your agent arranges a viewing with you, make a note of the buyer's name so that you can greet them by name when they arrive. Ask if the agent has any information them about them, as this will help you to decide what questions to ask during the viewing.

If more than one viewing has been arranged for a particular day, it does not matter if they overlap. If someone is interested in buying your house, they may be keener to put in an offer if they see other people are interested in it too. Also, if a buyer feels there may be competition for the house, the offer they make may be higher.

How should I prepare for a viewing?

Ensure the house is spotlessly clean and tidy

Your house will look bigger, more welcoming and more expensive if it is clean and tidy.

Pay particular attention to unpleasant smells

Check especially odours from pets, drains, toilets and fridges. Leave the toilet window slightly open for half an hour before the viewers are due, or place a lightly-scented potpourri in this room. You may also wish to introduce some pleasant smells, but avoid chemical-smelling air fresheners, as some people find these offensive and they can occasionally trigger asthma. Buyers may also suspect you are trying to mask a bad smell. Opinion is sharply divided on whether visitors will react favourably to fresh coffee and baking aromas, or whether they see straight through them as a ruse.

De-personalise your rooms

A buyer will be trying to imagine living in the house. Make this as easy as possible for them by putting away family photos, evidence of eccentric hobbies and the train set that has taken over the spare room.

If you've got it, flaunt it

Make sure all the good points about your property are on show. Most people remember things better if they have seen them, rather than just being told about them. So, if your driveway is large enough to accommodate two cars, try to make sure two cars are parked on it. If you have a wonderful log-burning stove, make sure there are logs crackling merrily on it.

'Make sure all the good points about your property are on show.'

Adjust the heat and ventilation

If the house is chilly, buyers will find it difficult to imagine it being comfortable to live in. Make sure the house is warm in winter, but not oppressively so. If the weather is very hot, make sure the house is well ventilated and airy.

Ensure calm

If possible, banish children and domestic animals for the period of the viewing. Your dog may be ecstatic to see the buyer and anxious to play, but the feeling may not be reciprocated. However much you love them, sometimes pets can be noisy, messy, smelly and distracting. A house without domestic animals (and associated smells and hairs) is more likely to appeal to a buyer, and you may even wish to consider boarding your dog with a relative or friend while the house is on the market and viewings are taking place.

Consider playing music

Less talkative visitors may be intimidated by the silence as they walk around. Consider playing quiet background music, but make sure it is a neutral, pleasant sound, without a heavy beat, as well as very quiet, so that it does not distract from the business on hand or impede conversation.

Arrive in good time

If you are not living in the property, try to arrive there half an hour before the viewing. Turn on the heating and the lights, check the property over, and clear any post from behind the door.

'Always stand back and allow the buyers to go in first. This will make the room seem both larger and more territorially neutral than if you enter first.'

Have utility bills to hand

Buyers may ask about how much the house costs to run, or what council tax bracket the property occupies.

In what order should I show the rooms?

Opinion among estate agents is divided on this. Some recommend showing the best room first, to get off to a good start, while others suggest saving it until last to end on a high. In practice, it will partly depend on the layout of your house, and partly on the inclinations of the buyer.

Whichever order you present the rooms, always stand back and allow the buyers to go in first. This will make the room seem both larger and more territorially neutral than if you enter first.

Let them take in the feel and appearance of the room and allow them to ask questions. If they remain silent, you may want to begin to point out the benefits and features of the room.

When you have shown them round, invite them to walk round on their own and indicate that you will be available if they have any questions when they have finished.

What questions should I ask the buyers?

You will want to find out the position of the buyer, and the following questions may be useful:

- Are you a first-time buyer?

- Do you have a mortgage arranged?

- How long have you been looking?

- Do you have a property to sell?

- Is it on the market?

- Have you had any offers?

- Why are you looking at this area in particular?

- Have you looked at many properties?

What questions am I likely to be asked?

Just as you want to find out the position of the buyers, they will want to find out why you are selling your house, so be prepared for them to ask.

If you are hoping to sell to move to a larger property, be careful how you phrase this. You do not want to imply that your property is too small. Similarly, if you are downsizing, you do not want to give the impression that your house is too large or expensive to manage.

When you are asked if there has been much interest in the property, try not to answer in the negative. If there has been little interest, try to be vague. If buyers feel nobody is interested in the property, they will expect to succeed with a lower offer.

Questions often asked by buyers include:

- Why are you selling?

- How long has the house been on the market?

- What are the neighbours like?

- Has there been much interest in the property?

- Are there any new building developments planned in the area?
- Has the house ever been flooded?
- Is there anywhere to park the car?
- How long have you lived here?

How can I 'sell' the good points of the property?

Mention hidden assets

If your house has a favourable feature that cannot be observed, e.g. loft insulation, be sure to mention it during the viewing.

Talk about what interests the buyer

Echo the sentiments expressed by the buyer, and take the opportunity to add something. If the buyer says, 'It feels like a warm house,' you might reply, 'Yes, I think it's the extra insulation. And we had a new boiler fitted six months ago. It's really efficient and has a two-year guarantee.'

Do your homework on other properties for sale in your area

The chances are that buyers will be looking at other similar properties, and you need to show them what your house offers that the other properties do not. However, avoid making a direct comparison, as you do not want to draw their attention to someone else's house.

Nowadays it is easy to research other local properties for sale on the Internet.

Relate selling points to use

For instance, rather than saying, 'There are worktop lights in the kitchen,' say, 'These kitchen worktop lights make it really easy to see what you're doing.'

Have solutions ready for problems

'Is the kitchen too small for a fridge?' Answer: There is a power point and a space in the utility room. 'Does the loft hatch have a built-in ladder?' Answer: No, but if you installed one there is enough space for it to come down . . . just here.

How can I deal with negative comments?

If the visitor makes a negative comment, don't become defensive, but be ready to turn it into a positive. A small garden can be described as 'easily managed', and you can point out that a house with small rooms is easy to heat. If there is simply no positive to be found, ('The window frames are rotting,'), as a last resort you could always fall back on, 'It's true they do need a bit of attention, but of course that's reflected in the asking price.'

Don't let your tongue run away with you. There may be aspects of the house you would prefer not to highlight, so, with regard to these, beware of answering questions the buyer has not asked.

Should I discuss the price?

Never allow yourself to be drawn into discussions on price during the viewing. If you have an agent, this is one of the things you pay them to do. Even if you are an experienced negotiator, you should not try to negotiate face-to-face, as you may make a verbal agreement that you later regret. Negotiations need to be carefully managed, preferably by a middleman (usually the agent).

Never ask the buyers if they are going to make an offer. It is not a question that buyers will expect at a viewing. At best they will find it startling, at worst it may scare them away.

'If the visitor makes a negative comment, don't become defensive, but be ready to turn it into a positive.'

How long can I expect a viewing to last?

The average amount of time a buyer spends looking around a house is astonishingly short – around 8-10 minutes. However, everybody is different and some buyers will want a longer viewing, whilst others will want to view the house more than once, maybe as many as 3 or 4 times.

You should allow the buyers to spend as long as they want looking round, but don't try to detain them when they have indicated they are ready to leave. Simply thank them for coming and say that you would be happy to see them again if they would like a second viewing or they would like to ask some more questions.

Summing Up

- Either you or your estate agent may conduct viewings.

- Always see buyers by appointment only.

- Allow plenty of time before a viewing to prepare the house so that it is looking its best. If you do not live in the property, arrive early to check it over and turn on the heating if needed.

- Allow the buyers to enter the rooms first, and let them take in what they see before you begin to talk.

- Decide what questions you may wish to ask the buyers. Consider what answers you will give to the questions most commonly asked by buyers.

- Mention the things that make your house special, but avoid freely volunteering information on potential disadvantages.

- Try to turn negative comments by the buyer into positives.

- Never discuss the price or ask buyers if they are going to make an offer.

Chapter Eight

Timing

It is possible that you have no control at all over when you sell your house. A change of employment, financial difficulties, the death of a relative, divorce, and many other things can force you to put your house on the market at an unfavourable time. However, if you have freedom to choose, it is worth considering whether good timing will help you sell your house more quickly or for a better price.

It is important to sell your house quickly. The longer a house remains on the market, the more buyers will suspect there is something wrong with it. At a time when prices are tending to remain static or fall, the asking price may have to be reduced if the house hangs around unsold for too long.

Some properties remain on the market for not just weeks, but months, or even years. Buyers may wonder what is wrong with such a property, and anyone thinking about making an offer on it will almost certainly imagine that the seller must be desperate to sell, and will reduce the offer accordingly.

'The best time to sell a house is in the spring. The worst time of year to try to sell is December and January.'

What is the best time of year to put a house on the market?

The best time to sell a house is in the spring. This is a time of year when change is in the air, and the improving weather makes people feel more inclined to get out and about and arrange viewings. People will have generally recovered from the Christmas bills, and many will be wanting to move in the summer, before the new school year begins.

The worst time of year to try to sell is December and January. Most people would not choose to move over Christmas, and January is a bad month financially for many people. Low light levels, bad weather and short days mean that your house will not be seen to its best advantage during viewings.

Surprisingly, August is also a poor time to sell, the main reason being that people are busy with holidays rather than moving house. If you can wait, delay until September, when the housing market picks up again. The autumn is a good time to sell, not as good as the spring, but better than August or during the worst of the winter.

However, houses do sell all year round, and if you are forced to put your property on the market at a time that is less favourable, do not despair. Make the most of your chances with good presentation and sensible pricing, and it is still likely that you can achieve a sale.

What is the best day to put my house on the market?

It is best to put your house on the market around the middle of the week. Weekends are the busiest time for viewings, and buyers who view your home on the first weekend will be aware that it has only been on the market for a couple of days. Even on the second weekend it will have been on the market for less than ten days, so you will stand a better chance of attracting an offer of the full asking price. After this, the chances of a full-price offer begin to drop.

At what point should I look for a new property to buy?

You will hold the strongest bargaining position on buying property if you are a cash buyer. Nowadays sellers are unwilling to get involved in house-buying chains, and before a seller will accept your offer you will normally have to show that any offer you make on a property is 'proceedable', i.e. you either have funds in the bank, a mortgage offer in place, or the sale of your house is underway. If your offer is not proceedable, the seller is likely to express an interest in your offer, but keep their home on the market.

Another problem with looking around too early is that you do not know exactly what funds you will have available. If you end up having to reduce the price of your house to sell it, you may end up with less money than you had anticipated.

The ideal time to begin looking for a new home is as soon as you have accepted an offer on your own house. At this point, only a cash buyer (i.e. someone with the necessary money already in their bank account) will be in a stronger position than you.

How long does the sale take after I have accepted an offer?

Obviously this varies from property to property, but some broad generalisations apply.

The absolute shortest time in which you can complete a sale is 7 days. This will only apply if you have sold your home to one of the 'quick buy' companies that were mentioned in chapter 5.

A house sale can take as little as 28 days. This quick turnaround time is often specified by the sellers in cases of bankruptcy, but otherwise is rare. However, a normal sale by private treaty, without any complications, takes around 6 to 10 weeks. This would usually apply where the parties concerned are reasonably prompt in turning around the paperwork they receive, and there are no unexpected legal difficulties.

'The ideal time to begin looking for a new home is as soon as you have accepted an offer on your own house.'

What is a chain and how does it work?

A house-buying chain is created when several linked sales are going through the legal processes simultaneously, and is created in the following way:

- Seller A puts his house on the market and accepts an offer.

- Seller A finds a house being sold by Seller B and put in an offer.

- Seller A's offer is accepted.

- Seller B finds a house being sold by Seller C and puts in an offer.

- Seller B's offer is accepted.
- Seller C is now begins looking for a house to buy.

The longer the chain becomes, the greater the chances of delay or collapse. Everyone in a chain has to exchange together and complete at the same time, and it does not take much to bring the whole process to a grinding halt.

If you are part of a chain, and you are buying as well as selling, the deposit you receive from your buyer can normally be used towards the house you are buying. In a longer chain, this means that the buyer at the start of the chain pays a deposit and it gets passed all the way up the chain to the seller at the top, whose solicitor will hold the money until completion.

What else can slow down my sale?

Significant delays are caused when a sale falls through. There many reasons why this can occur, ranging from a change in the buyer's circumstances, to the existence of hitherto unsuspected dry rot.

'Price the house realistically.'

If you are in the unfortunate position of having had a sale fall through, there is nothing you can do except begin the process all over again. However, to avoid it happening a second time, take a look at the reason why the sale fell through. If it was a problem with your property, you might want to see if it is possible to put it right before you re-market the house. Taking a break in the sale process also means that when you put your house back on the market it will once again appear as a new listing.

How can I speed up the sale of my house?

There are two areas where you may be able to speed up your sale: during marketing and during the legal selling process.

Marketing for a quick sale

Price the house realistically. 'Realistically priced' is the phrase estate agents use to indicate that your house represents value for money, that it is cheaper than similar houses in your area.

Offer incentives. You could offer to pay the buyer's stamp duty, or their legal fees.

It used to be an incentive to advertise a house as having 'no onward chain'. However, nowadays it is less and less common for transactions to be part of a chain, although you do still sometimes see houses advertised in this way.

Helping along the legal process

Apart from chasing up and down the chain, there is little you can do to oil the legal wheels. However, where you know certain documents will be required by the buyer, you can prepare these in advance.

Think back to when you bought the house, if that is how you came to own it. What were the things that held up your purchase? If you still have the purchase documents, you may find that some of these will be required by the new buyer so get them out ready.

The most important thing you can do to keep the process moving is to complete your parts of the paperwork promptly and return them to your solicitor without any delay, the same day if possible. Keep copies of everything you send out, in case any documents get lost in the post. During the legal process, papers bounce backwards and forwards between the buyer and the seller like a ball in a tennis match. If the ball is in your court, return it swiftly to the other side.

What is the best day to complete a sale?

You may not have control over this, particularly if your sale is part of a chain.

Most sales complete on a Friday. Buyers like this day because it means they can settle in over the weekend with minimum disruption to their working life. If you are moving to a new house upon selling your home, you may also consider this an advantage.

However, completing on a Friday has some disadvantages, including:

- It is a very busy day for solicitors, mortgage lenders and banks. Delays may occur because there are so many sales going through on the same day.

- Removals firms are busiest on Fridays, and may charge more for a Friday move.

- If something goes wrong, you will have to wait until Monday to sort it out. If you happen to be moving, you may end up with your furniture in a van over the weekend.

Thursday is a good day to complete a sale, because it is near the weekend, but without the disadvantages of a Friday.

If you really have to complete the sale on a Friday, and you are not superstitious, Fridays that fall on the thirteenth of the month are quieter than other Fridays.

Summing Up

- It is important to sell your house quickly. The longer a house remains on the market, the more buyers will suspect there is something wrong with it.

- The best time of year to put your house on the market is in the spring, and the worst time is in early December.

- It is best to put your house on the market around the middle of the week.

- The ideal time to begin looking for a new home is as soon as you have accepted an offer on your own house.

- House-buying chains can cause the sale to be delayed or to collapse.

- Consider taking your house off the market while you fix the problem that caused a sale to fall through.

- If you are keen for a quick sale, price the house realistically.

- You can speed up the transaction by turning around your paperwork promptly. Keep copies of everything.

- Most people complete their house sale on a Friday, but there can be disadvantages to choosing this day of the week.

Chapter Nine

The Paperwork Trail

If you are not a fan of paperwork, the amount involved in selling a house can be positively scary. However, although it is tedious, it is relatively straightforward.

What paperwork has to be done before the sale process begins?

Home Information Packs (HIPS)

If you talk to anyone who sold a home between 2007 and 2010, you may be told that you need a Home Information Pack. This is no longer the case for England, Wales and Northern Ireland, as the use of these packs was suspended on 21st May 2010.

In Scotland, a Home Report, which is a similar type of document, is still required, and there are more details about this in chapter 10.

However, when Home Information Packs were scrapped, one element was retained. This was the Energy Performance Certificate, which is still required.

Energy Performance Certificate

You cannot sell your house without an Energy Performance Certificate (EPC). This is a legal requirement. In Scotland the EPC has to be displayed somewhere in the house, and in the rest of the UK it has to be included in the sales particulars.

'You cannot sell your house without an Energy Performance Certificate (EPC). This is a legal requirement.'

The EPC has two parts, the first of which shows how efficiently the house uses energy, and the second shows where energy savings can be made.

To get an EPC, you must engage the services of an accredited domestic energy assessor. You can find such a person from the Landmark Information Group (at www.epcregister.com). If you do not have access to the Internet, you can also ask your local estate agent to recommend an accredited domestic energy assessor, or look in the business telephone directory.

The assessor will visit your house to do the assessment. Work that has been carried out, but cannot be seen (e.g. insulation in the walls) cannot be counted unless you have proof that it has been done, such as photographs and accompanying paperwork.

Your property may already have an EPC and, if it is less than 10 years old, it may still be valid. Information on EPCs is in the public domain, and is held on the EPC register, which is operated by the Landmark Information Group on behalf of the government.

However, if you have had any work done on the house that will improve its energy rating, such as insulation, a new boiler or new windows, it may be worth getting an updated Energy Performance Certificate to demonstrate the improved energy-efficiency of the house.

You may not need an EPC on your house if any of the following apply:

- It is a listed building.

- It is a stand-alone building that has a total useful floor space of less than 50 square metres.

- It is due to be demolished when the sale is completed.

- It is a house or holiday accommodation that is rented out for less than four months per year.

These conditions may be changed from time to time, so always check whether an exemption applies to your house at the time you are selling.

In Scotland, the EPC is part of the Home Report, which is produced by a member of the Royal Institute of Chartered Surveyors. An accredited energy performance assessor is therefore not able to produce a stand-alone Energy Performance Certificate for a property that is being sold, although they can do this for a property being put on the rental market.

Proof of your identity

Solicitors have a duty to ensure that they are not involved with attempts to launder money that has been obtained as proceeds of a crime. They do this by verifying your identity when you first instruct them, and will ask you to supply proof of your identity and your address.

All solicitors are bound by these regulations, and you should not feel upset or offended by being asked to prove who you are and where you live.

Your solicitor should provide you with an estimate for the work and there are a number of things that can cause it to be legitimately revised upwards. These can include:

- More than one title is involved.
- The title being unusually complex.
- More than one mortgage lender.
- More than two endowment policies.
- Additional documents required, such as Power of Attorney, Statutory Declarations or Trust Deeds.
- A long chain of buyers and sellers.
- Unexpected increases in disbursements beyond the control of the solicitor.

If the sale falls through, your solicitor will usually charge you for work they have already carried out on your behalf up to that point.

House survey

The buyer is highly likely to want a survey done on your house. This is usually arranged as soon as a selling price is agreed. If the survey highlights a problem that has not previously been noticed, such as rot, subsidence or damp, your buyer may try to negotiate a reduction in the price, to cover the cost of putting right the defect. This is normal and reasonable, and you should try to reach an agreement with the buyer. After all, if the sale falls through because of woodworm, it is likely that this scenario will be played out again with the next buyer.

The three stages of a sale

The buyer has made an offer and you have accepted it. The survey has been carried out, and everything is satisfactory. Now the serious paperwork begins.

The sale is split into three stages:

- The preliminary stage – Where the buyer organises finances, conducts searches on the property, examines the title deeds and asks the seller to provide other information required.

- Exchange of contracts – At which stage the buyer is legally bound to proceed.

- Completion of sale – Whereupon the buyer can take possession of the property.

Preliminary paperwork: who does what and when

What the seller's side does	What the seller's side and the buyer's side both do	What the buyer's side does
▪ The estate agent confirms the price in writing to the seller. ▪ The estate agent sends out a Memorandum of Sale to the buyer's and seller's solicitors. ▪ The seller's solicitor obtains proof of title from the Land Registry. ▪ The seller completes a property information form and a contents questionnaire. ▪ The seller's solicitor prepares a contract. ▪ The seller's solicitor sends to the buyer's solicitor the questionnaires, the title documents and the contract.	▪ The selling price is agreed. ▪ If the survey reveals previously unnoticed defects, the parties may renegotiate the selling price downwards. ▪ Queries are resolved to the satisfaction of the buyer. ▪ The seller and the buyer sign the contract.	▪ The buyer arranges for the property to be surveyed and/or valued. ▪ The buyer sends a copy of the survey/valuation to the buyer's solicitor. ▪ The buyer's solicitor checks the survey to see if it reveals previously unnoticed defects. ▪ The buyer arranges a mortgage. ▪ The buyer arranges for insurance to be available. ▪ The buyer's solicitor examines the paperwork and checks the title. ▪ The buyer's solicitor raises searches and sends any queries to the seller's solicitor.

Exchange of contracts: who does what and when

What the seller's side does	What the seller's side and the buyer's side both do	What the buyer's side does
▓ The transfer deeds are signed.	▓ Completion date agreed and confirmed by both solicitors. This is inserted into the contracts. ▓ The seller's solicitor and the buyer's solicitor send the contracts signed by the seller and the buyer to each other. This is know as 'Exchange of Contracts'. At this point the contract become legally binding. ▓ The deposit is passed from the buyer's solicitor to the seller's solicitor. ▓ Meter readings are taken and utility companies and the local authority are notified of the change of ownership.	▓ The buyer's solicitor requests the funds from the mortgage lender. The mortgage deeds are signed. ▓ The buyer puts insurance and life policies in place.

Need2Know

Completion day: who does what and when

What the seller's side does	What the seller's side and the buyer's side both do	What the buyer's side does
▓ The seller's solicitor notifies the seller that the payment has been received. ▓ The seller authorises release of the keys (usually via the estate agent). ▓ The seller's solicitor sends the deeds and transfer documents to the buyer's solicitor. ▓ The seller's solicitor pays off the mortgage and takes his fee, sending the balance of the money to the seller.	▓ The seller moves out and the buyer moves in.	▓ The mortgage lender releases funds to the buyer's solicitor. ▓ The buyer's solicitor transfers the balance of the selling price to the seller's solicitor. ▓ The buyer receives the keys. ▓ The buyer's solicitor pays any stamp duty due to the Inland Revenue. ▓ The buyer's solicitor registers the new ownership with the Land Registry.

What information do I have to supply to the buyer?

The Property Information Form and the Fittings and Contents Form

Your solicitor will send you two forms to fill in, designed to give detailed information about your house to the buyer. These are called The Property Information Form, and The Fittings and Contents Form. There is a national protocol scheme under which most sellers' solicitors operate, which means that the forms are standardised and nationally agreed.

You should be accurate and truthful when you fill in these forms, and be careful to avoid any ambiguity or misleading statements. The Property Misrepresentations Act 1991, makes it an offence to make false statements about the house you are selling, although you are not under any obligation to give any information about the physical condition of the property. It is up to the buyer to make arrangements to assess this, and it is normally done through the survey.

If there is a question on the form to which you do not know the answer, it is acceptable to say so. It may be that the person who sold the house to you did not know who was responsible for maintaining the left-hand boundary and during your ownership it has never arisen because a repair has not been needed. If the buyer is unhappy with this, they will say so, and the matter will be investigated, but this is better than guessing the answer.

The Property Information Form covers the following subjects:

- Boundaries and boundary features
- Disputes and complaints
- Notices and proposals of future developments
- Alterations, planning and building control
- Guarantees and warranties
- Council tax

- Environmental matters

- Formal and informal arrangements (e.g. for shared use of roads, boundaries or drains)

- Other financial charges

- Occupiers

- Transaction information

- Services (utilities)

- Connection to utilities

The Fittings and Contents Form, which is much shorter, has sections for:

- Basic fittings

- Television and telephone

- Kitchen

- Bathroom

- Carpets, curtains, light fittings and fitted units

- Outdoor area

Guarantees, warranties and certificates

Your house will be sold as a second-hand item. As such, the buyer will want to see any kind of guarantee or warranty that will give them confidence in their purchase. These may include, but are not necessarily limited to:

- A National House Building Council (NHBC) warranty for a house that is less than 10 years old.

- Copies of planning permission and building consent for any alterations you have made to the property.

- A damp or timber treatment guarantee.

- A solar panel guarantee.

- A boiler/central heating installation certificate and guarantee.

- A boiler service record.

- An electrical installation work certificate of compliance.

- Paperwork relating to any new appliance still within its guarantee period.

- Fenestration Self-Assessment (FENSA) certification on windows or glazed doors.

What is FENSA certification?

On 1st April, 2002, new regulations came into force regarding any new windows or glazed doors. The new regulations made window and door installations subject to local authority building control. Therefore, if your house has had new windows or glazed doors since that date, you will need to provide the buyer with either a Building Regulations certificate from the local authority or a FENSA certificate. You do not need both, as the FENSA certificate is evidence that your doors and windows meet the building regulations.

A FENSA certificate is provided by the installer of the doors and windows at the time of installation. It should contain the following information:

- The address of the property

- The number of windows/doors installed

- The date of installation

- The name of the installer and their FENSA registration number

FENSA documentation does not cover the following:

- Conservatories

- Porches

- New builds

- Extensions

- Repairs to glass

Title deeds

The title deeds of a house used to be a paper document, kept in the possession of the house owner, or by the mortgage lender if the house was subject to a mortgage. When you bought a house, you could look through the papers and see who had owned the house throughout the years.

Nowadays the title to the property is kept in electronic form by the Land Registry. You are sent a Title Information Document (TID), which is proof that you bought the property. However, the good part about this method is that if the TID is lost or destroyed, you need not panic, because the information is still on the Land Registry system.

If your house is subject to a mortgage, your lender may wish to hold the original Land Registry TID. If so, when you want to sell your house, you will have to apply to your lender for this document, so that it can be sent on to the buyer's solicitor, to prove that you own the property you are selling. If not, your solicitor will obtain proof of title from the Land Registry for you.

Exchange of contracts

The exchange of contracts marks the end of the preliminary paperwork and is the point at which the whole transaction becomes legally binding. Exchange of contracts is exactly what it says: your solicitor and the buyer's solicitor exchange the contracts that you and the buyer have signed.

Exchange of contracts is the time that the first money changes hands between the buyer and the seller: usually 10% of the agreed selling price, or sometimes the difference between the mortgage amount and the selling price. This money will not be refunded if the buyer then backs out of the sale. In addition, you, as seller, can also claim damages for any other losses you may have incurred as a result of the non-completion of the sale.

'The exchange of contracts marks the end of the preliminary paperwork and is the point at which the whole transaction becomes legally binding.'

Completion

Completion of the sale (usually just known as 'completion'), normally takes place two or three days after exchange of contracts. During those few days the buyer draws down their mortgage. The balance of the selling price is transferred to your solicitor and, when the solicitor's bank has received cleared funds, the house keys can be released to the buyer.

You are expected to have moved out of your house completely by the time this happens, and to have removed all rubbish.

Insurance

In the majority of contracts, it is stipulated that the insurance of the house is the seller's responsibility until completion. Many buyers choose to put insurance in place at exchange of contracts, but you should not rely on this. It is better to have too much insurance than too little and, as the gap between exchange of contracts and completion is normally no more than a few days, the cost of insuring your house for this short period of time will be very small.

You may have taken out Chancel Repair Insurance (against claims against you by the Church of England to repair the parish church) and, if so, it may cover future owners of the property. If this is the case, the documentation must be passed along to the buyer's solicitor for inspection. The same will apply if you have taken out a Residential Contaminated Land Insurance, an Absence of Easement Insurance (not being allowed right of way to your property), or any of a selection of other insurances that can be available to homeowners, depending on the individual quirks of their property. Check out what you have, and see if the buyer requires sight of it.

Paying off your mortgage

When your house is sold, unless you are transferring the mortgage to another property, the mortgage will be paid off, or 'redeemed'.

Once the completion date is decided, the mortgage lender will calculate the redemption figure based on this. Allow a few days for the figures to be produced.

Your solicitor will normally take care of your transactions with the mortgage lender. Technically, your solicitor is also acting on behalf of your mortgage lender as well as on your behalf, but you pay for this service, not the mortgage lender.

'Your solicitor will normally take care of your transactions with the mortgage lender.'

Summing Up

- Before you begin to market your house, you should have an Energy Performance Certificate.

- When you instruct a solicitor, you will be required to provide proof of your identity and your address.

- Your buyer will probably want to have a survey done of your house. The findings of the survey may affect the final price agreed.

- The sale has three stages: preliminary, when the buyer finds out all about the property; exchange of contracts, when a deposit is paid; and completion, when the balance of the money changes hands and the buyer takes possession of the property.

- You will be required to fill in a Property Information Form and a Fittings and Contents Form for the buyer's information. You will also have to supply any warranties, guarantees and certificates and insurances associated with your house.

- The buyer's solicitor will want to see proof that you own the house. Your title (ownership) is proved by your Title Deeds or by the Title Information Document issued by the Land Registry.

- You should make sure your property is covered by your insurance until completion.

- Once the sale is complete you will be able to redeem your mortgage, if you have one. Your solicitor will normally take care of this on your behalf.

Chapter Ten

Selling a House
in Scotland

The legal process of selling a property in Scotland is significantly different to that in England, Wales and Northern Ireland. There are historical reasons for this, as the present system has evolved out of an earlier bias towards selling homes through sealed bids. The information in this chapter is only about selling a property in Scotland.

In terms of the order in which the sale processes take place, the Scottish process more closely resembles sale by auction than a private or agent-led sale in the rest of the UK, and therefore seems to provide less uncertainty for the buyer and seller. The Office of Fair Trading says: 'Scottish buyers and sellers generally seem more satisfied with their experience than their counterparts in England and Wales.'

Solicitor estate agents

The traditional way of selling a house in Scotland is through a solicitor estate agent, who performs the dual function of both marketing the home and handling the legal and conveyancing side of the sale. Nowadays solicitor estate agents still handle around half of all private home sales in Scotland, with the rest being sold through non-solicitor estate agents (known in England and Wales simply as estate agents).

Whichever of the two you choose to use, you will need to involve a solicitor at an earlier stage than if you were selling a house in the rest of the UK. This is because offers are submitted in writing, usually by a solicitor, meaning the legal process begins earlier in the transaction.

'The legal process of selling a property in Scotland is significantly different to that in England, Wales and Northern Ireland.'

If you shop around, you may find that some solicitor estate agents offer a package deal for both selling and conveyancing, and this may be cheaper than buying the two services separately. But, as with any service, beware of choosing an agent based solely on cost.

It is rare in Scotland to have joint agency arrangements, as a high number of sales are dealt with by sealed bids.

The Home Report

In Scotland, before you can begin to market your house, you have to commission a Home Report. You will have to do this, even if you choose to sell privately without using an estate agent.

It is best to shop around before you decide on which Home Report provider you will use. You should consider not just cost, but which lenders will accept a report prepared by the provider you choose. The Royal Institution of Chartered Surveyors provides a directory of chartered surveyors free of charge.

The Home Report contains information to help the buyer decide whether to make an offer on the property. It is paid for by you, the seller, but both you and the buyer have a right to sue the surveyor for negligence, if the information it contains is not accurate. It consists of:

- A survey
- A valuation
- A property questionnaire
- An energy report

The survey

This eliminates the need for each potential buyer to have a survey done on your house. It tells buyers about the type, age and construction of the property (a structural survey), and also gives information about the local area. The survey follows a standard format that categorises each of 24 separate elements of the house, e.g. the roof and the windows. Category 1 means no action or repair is needed. Category 2 means that future repair or replacement will be needed, and the buyer will be wise to get estimates. Category 3 means that immediate repair or replacement is needed.

The valuation

This helps buyers decide what to offer for the house and is normally accepted by mortgage lenders. It is advisable to ask for a standard mortgage valuation report, which puts the information into the format that most lenders require. Where the sellers adopt an 'offers over' method of selling the house, the amount set is often the same as the valuation. The valuation should also provide information on the estimated rebuilding cost for insurance purposes.

The property questionnaire

This contains the same type of information that is required on the Property Information Form used in the rest of the UK. It also covers alterations to the house, guarantees and issues such as previous flooding or the presence of asbestos.

The energy report

This includes an Energy Performance Certificate, as required in the rest of the UK. It also includes information on running costs.

Other Home Report information

The Home Report should be no more than 12 weeks old when the property first goes on the market. Once the house has been on the market for more than 12 weeks, you may find buyers ask you to have the survey 'refreshed' to satisfy their lender that nothing has changed.

You or your agent should provide a buyer with a copy of the Home Report within 9 days of request. You cannot refuse to provide a copy unless one of the following applies:

'It is advisable to ask for a standard mortgage valuation report, which puts the information into the format that most lenders require.'

- You don't believe the buyer has enough money to purchase the house.

- You don't believe the buyer is serious about making an offer.

- You don't want to sell the house to that buyer. (However, you cannot discriminate against a buyer for any reason that is against the law.)

Reasons a Home Report may not be required include:

- Your house has been on the market continuously since before 1st December, 2008.

- Your house is brand new.

- Your house has been newly converted and has never been occupied in its converted state.

- Your house is simultaneously used for both residential and non-residential purposes.

- Your house is a seasonal holiday home that cannot be used all year round. If it is a holiday home that can be used all year round, a Home Report is required.

However, if your house falls into one of these categories, you still have to provide buyers with a valid Energy Performance Certificate.

Always check with your solicitor whether you need to provide a Home Report. If you fail to provide a Home Report when you are supposed to, there is a penalty charge, currently set at £500.

'There is a great deal of difference between an offer in Scotland and an offer in the rest of the UK.'

Sealed bids

This is the traditional way of selling a house in Scotland. Buyers are expected to formally notify the agent of their interest in a house. When a few notes of interest have accumulated, the seller and the agent agree a closing date and time within which offers must be made. When deciding on your closing date, remember you must allow enough time for buyers to arrange their finance.

Interested buyers will make their offers, and will hopefully base them upon the valuation in the Home Report and on the advertised 'offers over' amount. There is a great deal of difference between an offer in Scotland and an offer in the rest of the UK. In Scotland the offer is made in writing, and includes the price offered, the date the buyer wants to move in ('date of entry'), any additional items in the house the buyer wants to purchase, and conditions which will be specific to each purchase.

On the closing date you can decide which offer you want to accept. The offer you choose may not necessarily be the highest: there may be conditions in the highest offer that you do not want to accept. You are not obliged to accept any of the offers and you can choose to continue advertising the property. The whole process is rather like an auction conducted in writing.

If you do not receive many expressions of interest you may ask your agent to let it be known that you will negotiate with an individual buyer.

Accepting an offer and exchanging missives

When you decide to accept an offer, your solicitor will send a letter called a qualified acceptance. This says that you will accept the offer, but that you want some of the conditions of the offer changed.

After this there is an exchange of letters (called missives) between your solicitor and the buyer's solicitor, the purpose of which is to agree the conditions. Once you and the buyer agree on the conditions, a concluding missive is sent.

The concluding missive marks the point at which the agreement becomes legally binding. It is the equivalent of exchange of contracts in England and Wales.

Settlement

The settlement is when the sale is finalised, and is the equivalent to completion in the rest of the UK. Between the concluding missive and settlement, the solicitors will do the conveyancing, legally transferring the title, or ownership, of the property from you to the buyer. The buyer's solicitor prepares a document called the disposition, which transfers the title, and your solicitor will check and agree this.

Summing Up

■ The process of selling a house in Scotland is significantly different to that in the rest of the UK and provides greater certainty for the seller.

■ Solicitor estate agents perform the dual functions of both marketing the property and undertaking the conveyancing procedures. However, you can choose to use a non-solicitor estate agent and a separate solicitor if you wish.

■ In Scotland, before you can begin to market your house, you have to commission a Home Report. It contains information to help the buyer decide whether to make an offer on the property, and is paid for by the seller.

■ If your property falls into a category where you do not have to provide a Home Report, you will still have to provide an Energy Performance Certificate.

■ The traditional way of selling a house in Scotland is by sealed bids. On the closing date you can decide which offer, if any, you want to accept.

■ When you decide to accept an offer, your solicitor will send a letter called a qualified acceptance.

■ Your solicitor and the buyer's solicitor will then 'exchange missives', at the end of which the conditions of sale are decided to the satisfaction of you and the buyer.

■ The concluding missive marks the point at which the agreement becomes legally binding. It is the equivalent of exchange of contracts in England and Wales.

■ The settlement is when the sale is finalised, and is the equivalent to completion in the rest of the UK.

Glossary

Absence of Easement Insurance

An insurance against being denied right of way to your property.

Buyer's market

When there are more sellers than buyers.

Capital gains tax

Tax paid by a property seller on the profit made upon the sale of items that include a second or additional home.

Cash buyer

Someone who does not need a mortgage to buy a property, but who already has the money in their bank account.

Chain

When a series of property sales are each dependent upon one another.

Chancel repair liability

The liability on the part of some home owners to pay for repairs to their local church. Chancel repair liability insurance can be taken out to protect against this.

CHAPS payment

Clearing House Automated Payment System payment, which is an electronic money transfer between one bank account and another.

Completion

The point at which a house sale is finalised (in all of the UK except Scotland).

Conveyancing

The legal transfer of property ownership from one person to another.

Disbursements

Fees additional to solicitors' charges, incurred during conveyancing.

Domestic energy assessor

A person accredited to carry out an energy performance assessment and issue an Energy Performance Certificate.

EPC (Energy Performance Certificate)

Document showing the current energy-efficiency of a building and its potential energy efficiency if suggested measures are carried out.

Energy performance rating

The rating that a property is given on the Energy Performance Certificate.

Energy Performance Register

The official list of Energy Performance Certificates for properties in the UK.

Estate agent

Someone whose job is to broker property sales.

Exchange of contracts

The point at which a house sale becomes legally binding (in all of the UK except Scotland).

FENSA certificate

Fenestration Self-Assessment Certificate supplied by installers of windows and glazed doors.

Freehold

Where a property and the land it stands upon are owned by the same person.

Gazumping

When a seller accepts a second, higher offer on a property from a new buyer and cancels the sale previously agreed with the first buyer.

Gazundering

When a buyer lowers the offer price that has already been agreed.

Guide price

At auction, the price the property is expected to sell for.

HIP (Home Information Pack)

A collection of documents that was once a legal requirement when selling a house, but is no longer required.

Home Report

In Scotland only, a collection of legal documents that property sellers are required by law to make available to buyers.

Home staging

Furnishing and dressing up a house for the purpose of attracting buyers.

Kerb appeal

How attractive a property looks from the outside.

Land Registry

The official body holding details of ownership of property in the UK.

Leasehold

Where a property and the land it stands upon are owned by different people.

Licensed conveyancer

Professionals who have passed examinations that qualify them to act solely in matters related to the sale and purchase of property in England and Wales.

Missives

In Scotland only, notes or letters sent between solicitors to establish the conditions of a property sale.

Mortgage

Sum of money borrowed for a house purchase, where normally the house being purchased is used for security of the loan.

Mortgage redemption fee

A sum sometimes charged when a mortgage is paid back in full before the expected date.

Multiple agency

When two or more estate agents have a contract to market a property and the fee is only paid to the agency that introduces the buyer.

Negative equity

When the sum owed to the mortgage lender is greater than the sale value of the property upon which the loan is secured.

NHBC

National House Building Council.

OIRO

Offers in the region of.

Ombudsman

An official appointed to investigate individuals' complaints.

POA

Price on application.

Property portals

Internet websites that specialise in the sale of property.

Reserve price

At auction, the price below which a property will not be sold.

Sale by private treaty

The term used to describe a property sale that is not carried out by auction, but by private negotiation between two parties. Normal sales through estate agents are carried out by private treaty.

Sales particulars

A description of a property, often including photographs, a floor plan, a map and an Energy Performance Certificate.

Help List

Professional Organisations

The Financial Conduct Authority

www.fca.org.uk
25 The North Colonnade
Canary Wharf
London
EH14 5HS
Tel: 0800 111 6768
The Financial Conduct Authority regulates the standards and conduct of financial firms. You can use it to check if a firm is on the Financial Services Register.

The Law Society of Scotland

www.lawscot.org.uk/Public_Information
26 Durmheugh Gardens
Edinburgh
EH3 7YR
Tel: 0131 226 7411
lawscot@lawscot.org.uk
The Law Society of Scotland is the professional body for solicitors in Scotland. It will help you find a solicitor and also deals with complaints against solicitors in Scotland.

The Legal Ombudsman for England and Wales

www.legalombudsman.org.uk
Tel: 0300 555 0333
This is the body that resolves complaints about solicitors and lawyers in England and Wales. The website can be accessed in different languages, including Welsh.